Penguin Special

ON OUR CONSCIEN
The Plight of the Elderly

Jack Shaw is 34. He has a first-hand knowledge of
environmental problems in our cities and towns – his
mother's home in Halifax, where he spent his teens,
is in a slum clearance area. He has been in journalism
since he left a Halifax grammar school at 16, working
first for the *Halifax Courier* and then, after National
Service with the RAF in Singapore, he spent almost six years
with the Press Association on Fleet Street. Following
a year in Spain, writing a little and studying, he returned
to newspapers and joined the *Star*, at Sheffield, where
he now writes feature articles and leaders. Throughout
1970 he was the leader of a team of five journalists
investigating and reporting on social problems in Sheffield,
most of which concerned the old. This book takes its
title from the *Star's* campaign, which won for its editor,
Colin Brannigan, the IPC award for Campaigning
Journalist of the Year.

On Our Conscience

The Plight of the Elderly

Jack Shaw

Penguin Books Ltd, Harmondsworth,
Middlesex, England
Penguin Books Inc., 7110 Ambassador Road,
Baltimore, Maryland 21207, U.S.A.
Penguin Books Australia Ltd, Ringwood,
Victoria, Australia

Published in Penguin Books 1971
Copyright © Jack Shaw, 1971

Made and printed in Great Britain by
C. Nicholls & Company Ltd
Set in Linotype Pilgrim

Contents

Preface

'I don't want to live to spend another Christmas alone ...'
These sad words were spoken by a ninety-six-year-old widow, an
arthritic cripple, in December 1969, and were the inspiration for
an intensive year of investigation into the condition of the
elderly and the needy in the city of Sheffield. They were quoted
in a story published that Christmas by the newspaper which
employs me, *The Star*, Sheffield's evening newspaper. A discussion of the story dominated an editorial conference shortly before the year's end at which the editor and his closest advisers
considered some of the possible activities of the paper in 1970.
A decision was taken that any similar cases which were brought
to our attention would be thoroughly investigated. Every evening throughout the year we invited our readers to tell us of
needy cases. The response was both surprising and alarming.
Even in the summer months the number of new cases did not
fall below twenty a week and by the year's end 1,313 had passed
through our books. I found myself leading a team of four reporters who worked together inquiring into social problems for
twelve months. The vast majority of these problem cases concerned the old and the infirm, suffering as they so often do the
social distress of poverty, slum homes, lack of companionship,
mental infirmity and physical disability, and it soon became
quite clear that the extent of provision for the old in Sheffield
was not enough.

We set out to discover how and why services to the elderly
and the infirm were not adequate and, by drawing attention to
the more prominent aspects of the problem, to urge greater
action from the local authority, from voluntary organizations

and from the public, all of whom we hoped would be made more aware of and more responsive to one of the greatest social ills of our time.

It can be argued that journalism and sociological study have much in common. Our interest in the problems of the elderly came primarily from a journalistic standpoint, although on many occasions we felt the investigations we were conducting were more akin to social work than they were to journalism. Indeed, only a very small number of the cases we investigated were reported in the columns of *The Star*, leaving a store of useful, but unused, information. Similarly, many more facts and figures came to hand than could be incorporated in the necessarily short articles which appear in an evening newspaper. This book makes use of the information we recorded in 1970 as well as further research.

It is the contention of this book that the problems we encountered in Sheffield are typical of those to be found in most of the large urban-industrial areas of this country. I would expect similar investigation in, say, Leeds, Manchester, Birmingham or Liverpool to produce similar comments on services for the aged.

The plight of the elderly is a national problem and not something peculiar to Sheffield, where comparisons which I do not have sufficient information to make might prove that Sheffield gives better services than some other urban areas.

In writing this book I have used the Seebohm Report as the main basis for argument. This is at present the most authoritative document on local social welfare in existence. No other surveys or treatises which have been drawn to my attention are sufficiently recent, comprehensive or relevant. In fact, the whole subject of caring for the elderly suffers from a lack of detailed, statistical information, especially on a purely local basis – which is where it matters most. I hope that this book adds something to the sum of knowledge and to the arguments surrounding this subject. It is the nature of such Reports as that of the Committee on Local Authority and Allied Personal Social Services (Seebohm) that they are generalizations. Taking the City of

Sheffield as an example, I have tried to illustrate and make specific some of its general criticisms of the country as a whole and to show how, even when a local authority is concerned and anxious to improve its services to the old, they can, nevertheless, leave much to be desired.

Its campaign into the problems of the elderly won the Campaigning Journalists of the Year Award for *The Star*'s Editor, Mr Colin Brannigan, in the International Publishing Corporation's National Press Awards for 1970. In reaching a unanimous decision the judges said of the campaign, 'This involved mobilizing a considerable part of the paper's journalistic resources, sustaining a lengthy campaign with vigour and resource and ensuring that it was carried through to practical effect.'

I must place on record my gratitude to my colleagues, Danny Gallagher, who contributed an appendix to this book, Gordon Ducker, John Honeywell and Susan Dewar, all of whom personally investigated dozens of cases during 1970. Without their work this book could not have been written. I must also record my thanks to the Editor of *The Star* for his encouragement and constructive criticism during the writing of this book.

One

The Age
of Neglect

Advances in medical science, better nourishment and improved standards of public health have all contributed to prolonging human life. As a result the number of the elderly of the United Kingdom, at present about eight million, is steadily increasing.

There is nothing surprising about this increase: it has been predicted by census, and the need to make provision, not only for the present aged population but also for that of the future, has long been known. Yet, although in the era of the welfare state, we have failed to plan adequately for old people. Many thousands of them are still neglected by society, their final years grim and cheerless.

How and why have we failed the old? Is it because old age is an unpleasant topic, a threat which awaits us all? Is it because we are reluctant to admit the inevitability of old age; because, in the vigour of our youth, we prefer not to think that one day we too could be plagued with the stiffness of arthritic joints, that senility could befuddle our minds and that infirmity might make us dependent on others for our daily needs? When we look to a retirement that will release us from the strains of working life, we hide from the harsher realities of old age – realities that our society is too busy, or too selfish, or too preoccupied to give the needs of the elderly their rightful place in the order of priorities.

Consider the never-ending debate on the subject of youth. Continually the problems of young people, their education, their music, their drugs and their violence are surveyed, analysed, discussed and reported on. They clamour for attention and they have the energy to make themselves heard. Youth, high in spending power and loud of voice, has become a cult and its words and its slang have become part of our language. Old age, its antithesis, is not news.

In its devotion to the demands of the young our society has failed to listen to the weaker voice of the elderly and the problems of old age have made correspondingly less impact. There is a paradox in the fact that, in youth's demands for a better life and a better future, its marches in support of human rights and dignity rarely demand that the ultimate future, the final years of life, should be made easier. Here is a challenge for young people and a cause which requires the crusading vigour of youth.

It is a big challenge, for the unfortunate among the elderly are very many. They are those who live in slum back-to-back houses in the mean, littered streets of our industrial cities, managing without a bathroom, often without a kitchen and almost invariably without an indoor lavatory. The very amenities which would make life easier for them are the ones which they most often lack. Frequently these houses are running with damp and their landlords see no point in doing expensive repairs as they wait for compulsory purchase and the Corporation demolition men.

When rehousing does come it is usually the old who suffer most from the move. With old people's flats and bungalows in shorter supply than houses for families they can wait for months for a suitable vacancy. Often they are the last to leave a derelict, decrepit street and they live in fear as younger neighbours, companions and helpers, move out, and the windows of the houses all around are boarded up. The upsets and worries of changing the routine of a lifetime and moving into a new Corporation flat in a strange district or into an eyrie in a tower block bring more problems for them, with which the social services are ill-equipped to deal.

Many other old people need places in old folk's homes. They cannot get them. Fruitlessly, sometimes for months, sometimes for years, their doctors bombard the local authority with medical evidence and requests that an elderly patient who lives alone be taken into this kind of care. The wait for a place in an old folk's home can be so long that when it is finally offered the old person is debarred from taking it by increased infirmity and needs not a place in a home but a geriatric bed in hospital. But the provision of geriatric beds is inadequate for the numbers who require hospital treatment and there is even a class of old people who live in a limbo between old folk's home and geriatric bed. No one wants them. Senility or incontinence can make a local authority reluctant to give them a place in an old folk's home, but they are neither so senile nor so infirm that they need continuous geriatric nursing in hospital. The result is that they are left at home, dependent on neighbours and visits from home helps and health visitors, in no way properly able to care for themselves in the long periods they spend alone.

This, of course, puts a strain on local authority welfare services, which, for many years, have pursued policies designed to 'keep old people in their own homes' and to 'preserve their independence'. While this policy is motivated by a humane desire to do what seems best for the elderly, it is now open to criticism because it is questionable whether this is a real preservation of independence. Changing circumstances would appear to have invalidated it to some small degree.

The numerical difficulties of adhering to this policy are considerable and are not easing. Local authority social services attempt to cope with cases of the elderly in need which come to their attention, but a national shortage of welfare officers of all kinds often leaves such services undermanned and overstrained, with a peak work-load in the winter months when old people most need the services of social care officers, health visitors, district nurses and home helps. The result is that many old people do not get the help and assistance that they vitally need.

Poverty is a constant worry for the aged. Modern definitions of poverty say it is living below the norm for the community and therefore it need no longer evoke a picture of ragged clothes, unwashed bodies and near-starvation. But for many old people dependence on pensions and supplementary benefits when faced by constantly rising prices means gradually giving up the tit-bits of food that add variety to diet, buying cheaper or smaller cuts of meat or going to bed to keep warm under the blankets instead of expending fuel. Perhaps the problem is best illustrated by the fact that elderly people are often forced to buy solid fuel for their fires by the weekly bag. If winter ice and snow prevent the coalman from making his regular call they can run out of fuel and be in danger of dying from cold in an unheated house.

Perhaps the worst problem of all for the old is desperate, soul-sapping loneliness. Often they live solitary lives, without relatives or friends, shunned or forgotten by the world until they believe – and perhaps with justification – that no one cares. And when they do need help they do not know where to turn. Often their requests are held up indefinitely by the slow workings of bureaucracy.

A numerical assessment of the problems facing the elderly was given by Help the Aged, a national charity, in its annual report for 1969. It said that 350,000 old people lived without the use of a bath, kitchen or indoor lavatory ; 2,000,000 had access only to an outside WC ; 1,500,000 lived alone, and 300,000 were in urgent need of flats with some sort of supervision. On the subject of poverty this report stressed the danger of hypothermia (a fall in body temperature to a dangerously low level), and it remarked that at present levels of retirement pensions and supplementary benefits it was difficult to see how old people could remain warm and well-fed.

There is no reason to doubt that these figures are a fair illustration of the size of the physical problems we have to tackle on behalf of the elderly and they are sufficient to show that the provision of proper community care and companionship is a daunting task. Indeed, it is a problem of such magnitude that we are afraid to tackle it, and our mental dislike of accepting that we will one day grow old is, perhaps, a psychological barrier which leads us to treat old age as a problem which, if ignored, will go away.

But it will not go away, and although the problem of putting a decent roof over the heads of the old might decrease as stocks of council flats increase and more old folk's homes are built, changes in the structure and habits of our society are presenting new problems to the aged. Again, we have been aware of these social changes for some time and many of them are so obvious that they do not need the probing of teams of sociologists to bring them to light. But while we constantly ask how these changes will affect the younger generations, few have studied their effects on the old, and when they have their findings have made little impression on the general body of opinion in this country. In particular, those with the political power to alter policies in the light of a changing social structure have frequently failed to do so, with the result that the neglect of the old continues. Many politicians seem to forget that it is just as easy for an old person to be neglected in a modern council flat as it is in a slum, and, although throwing out the periodic financial sop of a few shillings on pensions might ease some political consciences, it does little to solve the deeper problems of old age and, in any case, it is never enough to relieve the financial strain of an ever-rising cost of living.

In our large towns and cities whole communities are being uprooted and dispersed by slum clearance, as they have been for some time. But it is the elderly who find it hardest to come to terms with this upheaval and only now are we beginning to realize the full social implications of these moves. Slum communities, although they lack bathrooms and inside toilets, are often neighbourly places where it is usual to keep a friendly eye on the old couple next door, to give them a hand with the shopping, to help with heavier household tasks and to visit regularly for a chat and a cup of tea. Research has shown that loneliness among the old is much more likely to be a cause for concern in new estates and blocks of flats than in these old slum communities which have developed their human relationships over many years. From the point of view of keeping people in contact with each other a slum has advantages over modern housing development. People live side by side in close proximity and look across a narrow street at each other's front doors and windows. A change in normal routine is quickly spotted and if an

15

old person doesn't bring in the milk bottle by the usual time a neighbour will soon suspect illness, or worse. Modern housing has greater respect for people's privacy. This is not wrong in any way, but it detracts from the kind of watchful neighbourliness which can be such help and comfort to old people.

Many of the modern estates are slow to develop as communities. Old people, set in their habits and accustomed to the same friends and neighbours, often do not take kindly to moving from the city centre to its outskirts. When the local authority rehouses them they frequently find it hard to adjust to their new surroundings and they miss the sense of community they previously enjoyed. Progressive local authorities encourage the formation of community associations when new estates are in their infancy but, even so, a sense of belonging takes a long time to develop and is especially difficult for the old to achieve when they know they are in the last years of their lives. Straggling estates of council semi-detached houses, especially those built before the war, often seem to have the worst community problems. Modern estates and flat developments have, to some extent, recognized the need for establishing a sense of community through their design.

One sociological change which has had a considerable effect on the provision of care for the elderly is the greater movement of families away from their roots. Many sons and daughters no longer live near to their ageing parents. Once the pattern of life was to live and work in the area of one's birth. Now sons and daughters are no longer tied by lack of money, lack of mobility and the need to work there. They move to suburban estates in the same town or their work takes them to other towns and cities. The effect, in a small or great degree, is to put distance and travelling time between themselves and their parents and render the task of filial care of the elderly more difficult. Then, too, more married women go out to work and the tradition that wives and daughters see to the comforts of aged parents and in-laws is being broken. The pressure of their working lives and the needs of their own families prevent them from taking the responsibility of taking care of aged parents. In many cases they are relieved to have the excuse. The words, 'I can't look after them, I've got to work and I've got my own children', are now a frequent excuse from a working wife, and increasingly there is a general feeling that it is the State or the local authority, and not sons and daughters, which should be responsible for the housing and comfort of the old. Many are only too glad to hand over to the State and the local authority what was once regarded as a duty; they demand that public welfare services should be responsible. Undoubtedly, a breakdown in the family as an integral unit is responsible for a great deal of the fears and the problems of the aged today.

However, it is also fair to say that part of the demand on the welfare services is for better facilities, because people know that the rudimentary help they can give aged and infirm parents is not enough, while once they would have been satisfied that it was the best that could be done. There are also many sons and daughters driven to the verge of nervous exhaustion from unrelieved care for an aged, infirm and cantankerous parent. Here again there is a problem. When an old person is in continuous ill health, or senile, care can be a twenty-four-hours-a-day, seven-days-a-week task. Those who accept this duty have a right to expect some periodic relief to take a well-earned holiday, but all too often they find it impossible to get a short-stay bed in hospital or a place in an old folk's home for the parent or partner concerned.

There are many reasons for the current neglect of the elderly. But for whatever reason, be it neglect by their children, by the local authority, the Welfare State, the community, or even their own independent refusal to accept that they are no longer capable of caring for themselves, far too many old people live lonely lives, devoid of human contact until their homes and their own physical and mental condition gradually deteriorates.

This deterioration is widely described as 'self-neglect', an expression which is often given as the reason for death from malnutrition in coroners' courts. 'Self-neglect' sums up society's lack of concern for the old; it is an excuse because it blames an old person who is probably quite incapable, either physically or mentally, of caring for himself or herself. It puts no stigma on society and absolves us from inquiring what degree of loneliness, what infirmity, or what extent of senile decay has led to an old person's decline. And when investigating the plight of the elderly nothing is more irritating than to hear otherwise responsible citizens comment: 'Well, it's self-neglect. There's nothing you can do about that.' Instead we should say that society is neglectful in that it has failed those against whom the charge of self-neglect is levelled.

The expression 'self-neglect' tells us something else about our attitude to the elderly. It exemplifies the general level of ignorance about the problems which face old people. If more people were truly aware of the horrifying conditions in which some old people live and more knowledgeable about the difficulties they face there would be much more response to appeals on behalf of the elderly and more progress would be made.

Such appeals have been made before and in Sheffield in 1965, in his pamphlet 'The Old Age Problem', Mr Arnold Freeman, who has spent most of his eighty-odd years campaigning for the social welfare of people, condemned our society in these words:

While they were young and able to work they put the community into their debt; that debt we are not honourably discharging. They helped to build the affluent society we are now enjoying; but they are being dishonestly deprived of the affluence they created.

In another pamphlet in 1967, which was endorsed by Sheffield's civic leaders and Members of Parliament, Mr Freeman called for old people's welfare groups to be set up in every part of the city.

An old person tends to sink into what is almost a sub-human condition of inner loneliness, boredom, apathy. If we can see into his innermost being we should see what he is asking for – more than for pensions, housing and medical assistance – is understanding and sympathy.

Mr Freeman is a man held in the highest esteem in Sheffield for his work with the Sheffield Educational Settlement and the Sheffield Abbeyfield Society, which is concerned with housing old people. It is disturbing therefore that the warning words of an eminent man whose opinions are highly respected in his home city should have little, if any, effect on its political leaders – even those who endorsed his pamphlet. His 1967 pamphlet 'New Worlds for the Old' put the situation plainly enough when, speaking of the shortage of voluntary recruits to help the old, he wrote:

These difficulties exist at the present time because we have not yet woken up to the urgency of the old age problem. We are relying on haphazard, fragmentary efforts. We need as a city to become deeply and comprehensively conscious of what is required. If we can be given an imaginative civic lead; if there is sufficient skilful publicity, there would be no difficulty about recruiting helpers.

But at that time no determined action was taken. In 1965 he asked:

Would it be possible to bring into existence a small group of young persons of very high ability, who would make it their sole concern to get something fundamental and far-reaching done about the problem of old age?

He too noted the lack of a powerful voice to demand a better future for the elderly:

An article in *The Times* of a few months ago made this remark 'The care of the aged suffers from the lack of a young vociferous group such as advocates more roads or better education: instead it hides in the back street'.

It has become quite obvious that a better deal for the aged must be preceded by greater appreciation of the problems from the general public. This would lead not only to greater interest in voluntary help but also to sufficient political pressure to bring about change.

This book, therefore, is intended not only to describe by detailed example the condition of some of the unfortunate among the elderly, to look at the different factors relating to their care and to draw conclusions, but also to show how, through the pressure of publicity and by arousing the public conscience, changes can be brought about.

The problems encountered in Sheffield, the fifth largest city in England, are typical to a greater or lesser extent of those to be found in every city and town in the country. This is not intended to be a statistical survey ; nor is it intended to draw comparisons with other cities and towns which might be proved invidious. Despite the awful nature of some of the cases found in Sheffield, nationwide comparisons, which the research for this book does not entitle me to make, might well prove that Sheffield makes comparatively better provision for old people, in some respects, than other major cities.

Nevertheless, some shocking examples of society's neglect of the elderly were discovered in Sheffield, some of them seemingly inexcusable.

Two

Enlightened City –
Geriatric Slum

Sheffield is a vital modern city, yet one which its local spokesman at the British Medical Association described as a 'geriatric slum'. Such a description comes hard on a city which, it is fair to say, has enjoyed enlightened civic rule for many years. It is this rule which has totally changed the physical appearance of the city and brought many social benefits to its population of almost 530,000 people, of whom an estimated 75,000 are elderly.

Physically, Sheffield can now boast of its attractions as a place to live ; once it lived up to the very worst traditions of the old Yorkshire adage of 'where there's muck, there's brass'. Its fame as a producer of quality steel is centuries old, but, in common with other centres of industry, the population and urban area of the city saw rapid growth during the Industrial Revolution to leave a legacy of nineteenth-century slums and dereliction. Until fairly recent times hundreds of small furnaces and foundries pumped fumes and filth into its atmosphere and to this day the name of Sheffield is almost as synonymous with smoke as it is with steel.

Contemporary accounts of Sheffield in the middle of the last century contain horrifying descriptions of the filth of streets and rivers. Public services and facilities would be described as non-existent by today's standards and life expectancy was so short that there was no old age to become a problem – except, of course, that old age began early. File grinders, for example, filling their lungs with dust, could expect an average life span of thirty-five years. The air of the city was so polluted that to this day there persists a tradition of snuff-taking to clear the nasal passages of atmospheric filth, and the East End of Sheffield, where most of its great steelworks are ranked together, even has its own highly individual accent – a peculiarly nasal version of the dialect of south Yorkshire, spoken through the nose as if its users are afraid to open their mouths for fear of what they might breathe in. Sheffield recognized the health danger of this atmospheric pollution before the turn of the century and although accent and tradition continue the reason for them has been removed by one of the most progressive clean-air policies in the world. This is perhaps the best example of Sheffield's enlightenment for, at a time when pollution of the environment is arousing worldwide indignation, Sheffield is able to boast the cleanest air of any comparable city in Europe. Respiratory complaints, a scourge in industrial cities, will no doubt exact a lesser toll in Sheffield in future as a result.

Architecturally, modern Sheffield is an exciting city. Like Rome, it stands on seven hills which present dramatic views from towering blocks of flats. Slum clearance began early in this century and by the late 1920s its first big Corporation housing estates were well under way. More estates were developed during the thirties, and after the Second World War Sheffield renewed its attack on the slums and almost completely redeveloped a city centre which was badly damaged by German bombs in December 1940. It is claimed that this city centre now contains one of the finest and most extensive shopping areas in the North of England.

Since the war slum clearance has gone on at great speed, although a great deal still remains to be done. But the result of a rolling building programme for rehousing has meant a continuous expansion of the number of houses owned by the Corporation. This policy and its results have been the envy of many other authorities and some of Sheffield's fine new estates and tower block developments have been heaped with praise, some of which, particularly in relation to the design of flats for old people, is, I feel, without foundation.

Of especial architectural interest is the Gleadless Valley Estate, a combination of houses and low-rise flats built in a country setting on steep hillsides, where, it was said, such a development was impossible; Norfolk Park, where tall blocks dominate the skyline, and Sheffield's three giants, the Park Hill, Hyde Park and Kelvin developments, three enormous and controversial blocks of flats about which a great deal more must be said in later chapters.

The result of this far-reaching clearance and rehousing programme is that the Corporation has become by far Sheffield's biggest landlord with over 70,000 houses and flats to which new building now adds more than 2,000 dwellings a year. Therefore, the city has made itself responsible for a very large number of people under its own roofs and, although no criticism is intended of the social benefits of this policy, it has nevertheless created a climate in which people tend to be less dependent on themselves and look more and more to the Corporation to provide them with a home as a right.

In its housing for old people, however, Sheffield has much less to boast about and one can only conclude from the available evidence that the proportion of this massive effort which has been devoted to the needs of the elderly has not been enough; and that in many cases the quality of accommodation provided for the old has been too low.

A great deal more will be said about housing the elderly in later chapters of this book but it is enough to say at this stage that Sheffield applies descriptions such as 'purpose-built' to old people's flats which seem to disregard the needs of the old and the infirm; that the wait for such a flat can, apart from slum clearance cases, be many years; and that at the beginning of 1970 Sheffield had in existence only one sheltered flatlet scheme, despite the fact that the value of such schemes has long been proven, and that Sheffield's one scheme was such a success as a social experiment in housing the elderly that the need for more should have been acted on earlier.

Welfare services for the elderly have shown continuous expansion over the years, but in its provision of residential homes for the aged Sheffield has lagged behind. Ministry of Health figures showed that at the beginning of 1970 Sheffield's provision of places per thousand of elderly population was the worst for any major city in the country. At that time twenty old folk's homes provided 740 residential places. Nor would the position improve much in future. In 1965 Sheffield provided 11·2 places in residential homes per thousand of elderly population, compared with a national average of 15·6 per thousand. A projection to 1971 raised the Sheffield figure to 13·4, by which time the national average would have risen to 20·2.

The problem for the local Health and Welfare Department was getting loan sanctions from the Government to build homes. Had Sheffield started a larger building programme for old folk's homes many years earlier the position would not have been so serious and loan sanctions for a larger programme might have become a more routine matter. As it was, Sheffield was in the position of having to fight to get loan sanctions to build two such homes a year.

On the other side of the coin Sheffield has a home-help service more numerous and costly than the average. Local health service statistics issued by the Institute of Municipal Treasurers and Accountants and the Society of County Treasurers in March 1969 showed that Sheffield spent thirty per cent above the national average on this service. This was borne out by a Government Report, 'The Home Help Service in England and Wales' by Audrey Hunt, published by the Stationery Office in April 1970, which showed Sheffield employed about nine hundred home helps and that more than ninety per cent of their clients were elderly – figures which led to claims that Sheffield provided the best such service in the country. Nevertheless, this service was, and is, stretched to the limit.

These figures illustrate the emphasis which Sheffield has placed on the policy of 'keeping old people in their own homes' and the question must be asked whether the right balance has been struck between domiciliary services and residential care. The contention of this book is that, despite the compassion which is shown in Sheffield's welfare services policy towards the old, it has been overweighted towards 'preserving their independence', leaving many who need the intensive care of a residential home to suffer in their own, often inadequate, houses.

Considering that the waiting list for places in old folk's homes, which was 900 in July 1968, had risen to 1,079 by October 1969, of whom over 300 were classed as being in immediate need, it was clear that urgent action would have to be taken. By early 1971, the figure had decreased to a total of 955, of whom 352 were classed as being in urgent need.

But it must also be recorded that only after press publicity and criticism of this situation did the Corporation make what can only be described as emergency application for loan sanctions to increase its building programme for old folk's homes.

It was also a fact that at the beginning of 1970 Sheffield's Social Care Department was overstrained due to high case-loads and staff shortages and that the Personnel Services Sub-Committee had twice deferred authorizing new appointments.

Bearing all this in mind it is hardly surprising that some of Sheffield's politicians and officials would be disturbed, and to some extent offended, when, at the beginning of 1970, *The Star* began to investigate and expose the shortcomings of the city's welfare and housing services for the aged.

Politically, Sheffield is a Labour Party stronghold. With the exception of the municipal year beginning in May 1968, the Socialists have controlled Sheffield for forty-three years. In January 1970 they were not unnaturally sensitive to any criticism of their administration because the coming municipal elections in May promised to be one of the closest contests in the city's history.

In May 1969, against all national trends, Labour regained the city from the Conservatives but their power rested on a flimsy base. They were still outnumbered forty-one to thirty-nine on the floor of the Council Chamber and held control through a slim majority of elder statesmen on the Aldermanic Bench. After the election of councillors in May 1970 the three-yearly election of half the aldermen would take place and the majority of councillors would dictate the future strengths of the respective parties on the Aldermanic Bench. It meant that the preservation of the status quo was not good enough for Labour. They had to win at least three seats to be sure of staying in power. With national opinion polls predicting a Tory landslide at a General Election, Labour could not view local prospects with equanimity at the beginning of the year.

It meant that the ruling party had to react both with words and decisions to revelations about the condition of old people in Sheffield. It is perhaps fair comment on their reaction that in the end Labour retained power handsomely in Sheffield and secured their position for some years to come.

This then is a brief description of Sheffield, its politics and its services for old people as they were at the beginning of 1970 when, after exposure of a horrifying example of a neglected old person, a point of crisis was reached.

Three

At Risk

On 1 January 1970, *The Star* was telephoned and asked if it 'could get anything done' for an old woman said to be living in squalor and neglect in a nearby Corporation tenement. Aged eighty, she lived alone in conditions which, without exaggeration, can be described as horrifying. But, because of the newspaper's intervention and insistence, she was removed to the safety and comfort of an old folk's home before the end of the afternoon. The case exemplified the depths to which an old person can sink through loneliness, senility and neglect, and dramatic press exposure brought home to the public of Sheffield that here was a problem which could not be ignored.

The old woman's deterioration was such that her condition was desperate. She was found slumped in a broken, urine-saturated armchair in front of an empty firegrate. The day was bitterly cold and she had no fuel for the fire and no other means of heating. Nor had she any food. She gazed from blank, uncaring eyes and gave all the appearance of waiting for death to overtake her.

Her person was filthy, face and hands showing embedded dirt. Her hair was lousy and her clothing foul rags. There was no change of underwear or winter clothing in the flat and it was obvious she had not changed the clothing she wore for a very long time.

Her three-roomed flat was in a disgusting condition, its walls covered in soot and dirt, streaked with excreta and hung with cobwebs. The living-room was the only room which was used, where the old woman slept on a chair in front of the fire. (This is a distressingly common habit among old people when they have unheated bedrooms or when they can only afford to keep one room warm.) It was a gloomy, stale-smelling place and every stick of furniture was thick with dust and grime. There were no carpets and the floor was encrusted with coal dust. Curtains to the living-room windows, giving on to a landing of the tenement block, were ragged and dirty and the windows so filthy that it was hardly possible to see through them into the dark room. The food cupboard by the side of the fireplace was quite bare, nor had she clean cutlery or usable crockery.

In the bedroom was a double bed, unused for a long time, its mattress so deformed and broken as to be impossible to sleep on. There were no sheets or blankets and the bed was thick with dust. In that room were some faded newspapers, a badly broken dressing table, which she had tried to smash for firewood, a wooden chair and, on the mantlepiece, two dust-covered china dancing girls. The kitchen was hung with cobwebs and its cold-water sink was blocked with four inches of dirty water in the bottom. There was a jumble of sour-smelling milk bottles underneath and one full bottle of sour milk on the draining board. A pitted, filthy water boiler was filled with rubbish, but the greasy old gas cooker was in working order. The lavatory, outside on the landing, was too foul to use and the coal-bunker beside it was bare of even a scraping of slack coal.

The wiring of the flat was found to be too dangerous to allow an electric fire to be connected to give the old woman some warmth while she waited for an ambulance.

Her personal possessions amounted to two bars of chocolate – the only nourishment which could be found – a new pinafore she had bought herself for Christmas, a pair of shoes, bought by her son and daughter-in-law, her rent book, her pension book, an insurance policy and some money in an old tobacco tin.

After eighty years of life this was the sum total of her possessions and she seemed without hope and without reason to carry on living. Although she was not ill in the medical sense, in her weak and underfed condition a continuation of her deterioration, without food and warmth, made her a candidate for a cold and lonely death. How much longer she could have survived was a matter for conjecture, but it could not have been for very long. No one who saw her on the afternoon of 1 January had the slightest doubt that she needed immediate care and that delay would be dangerous.

As it was, coal was borrowed, a fire was lit, she was fed hot soup and an ambulance called to take her to an old folk's home where she was bathed and deloused and a process of rehabilitation began.

The case highlighted communal and family responsibility and also posed questions about the work of Sheffield's Health and Welfare and Housing Departments, the need for early identification of such cases of neglect and the difficulties welfare workers have in persuading some old people to accept their help.

Firstly we must look at the question of identifying such a case. The urgent alarm was sounded by a cafe manager whose premises were across the street from the old woman's flat. He was also able to supply information about the woman's habits and her way of life.

He and his staff had known the old woman for about a year and she made what he described as 'set-your-clock-by-her' visits to his cafe at 11.30 each morning to buy fish and chips. She never bought anything but fish and chips and attempts to persuade her to vary her diet always failed. He said they came to realize after a while that fish and chips were her only food. 'We've seen her condition deteriorate, particularly over the last few months. She was getting dirtier and dirtier . . . you could see she wasn't being looked after,' he said. Because the cafe closed on Sunday, on Saturday 27 December they had given her an extra helping of fish and chips in the hope that she could warm them up for her Sunday meal.

He became concerned when she did not appear 'on the dot' at 11.30 a.m. on Monday 29 December, and when she still did not come the next day he sent one of his assistants across the street to the flat to see if the old woman needed help. The assistant returned in tears after seeing how the woman lived, but then went back with hot food.

When she did not come again on Wednesday 31 December

he telephoned Sheffield Social Care Department. On Thursday 1 January a meals-on-wheels van arrived, but the old woman could not eat the food that was brought. Indeed, according to the cafe manager, there was some argument about whether it should be left because she had no plate on which to put it and eventually it was left in its container. The cafe manager tried to telephone Social Care again because he thought that a great deal more ought to be done for the old woman than just the provision of meals on wheels. He could not get through and telephoned the newspaper instead.

The old woman's distressed and neglected condition might also have been brought to the attention of the welfare services by the rent-collector. Her flat, only a matter of yards from the modern city centre of Sheffield, was Corporation property and a collector called every Thursday for her £1 12s. 6d. rent. Even if he received the money at the door, one look at the grimy exterior of the flat and the ragged curtains at the window, and the woman herself, should have aroused suspicion. Alderman Harold Lambert, Chairman of Sheffield Housing Committee, was to point out, after seeing the flat a few days later, that one of the reasons why the Corporation persevered with the collection of rents door-to-door was to liaise with tenants, and collectors did have instructions to report such cases to the welfare services. He promised a complete reappraisal of what he termed Sheffield's 'early-warning system' for discovering elderly people in council property who might be in need, but added, reasonably enough : 'Even with the best intentions in the world one is going to find some error of judgement, some slip-up.'

Alderman Lambert was appalled by what he saw at the flat – 'I have seen my share of bad places, but I can honestly say I have never seen a place in that condition' – and as a result an immediate review of the duties of rent-collectors took place.

At the time the Chairman of the Housing Committee reiterated the Council's policy towards the elderly : 'Our concern is two things. One is preserving their independence and encouraging them to live in their own homes ; secondly, to offset their loneliness.' But he added an important comment on society and the role of the welfare services: 'I think it is wrong for people to abrogate their responsibilities. There is a family responsibility which is paramount. Public services are given to support this responsibility.'

A matter which was the responsibility for the Housing Department was the state of the electric wiring in the flat. This was discovered while the old woman was waiting to be taken to the old folk's home. In an attempt to keep her warm, an electric fire was brought in, but no power point could be found and, in any case, the wiring was thought to be too unsafe to attempt to make an emergency connection. This opinion was never contested by the Corporation and there is no need to emphasize the danger to an aged person living in an old property where the electrical installation is not safe.

A further point is that many of the fifty-six flats in the block, which was built in 1903, and those in a similar block across the street, are occupied by elderly people. They lack the kind of amenities old people most need. There are no bathrooms and the lavatories are outside on the landings. Some have been improved and fitted with 'mini-baths' but their design does not lend itself to improvement. At best they can be described as grim and forbidding and provide a poor environment for old people. Most of the residents were under the mistaken impression that they were condemned and would be demolished in due course; inquiries to the Housing Manager revealed that this was not the case. Knowing that most people living in such surroundings are old one would have expected the Health and Welfare Department and the Housing Department to have kept a closer watch on them. Only a matter of days before we learnt of this case another old woman, with a blind and deaf husband, died from vitamin deficiency in the block across the street, and a coroner's verdict of death from 'self-neglect' was recorded. This case led the Sheffield and District Coroner, Dr Herbert Pilling, to appeal to people to keep a watchful eye on their elderly neighbours and report cases of distress to the welfare services.

However, even conceding errors of judgement or lack of knowledge on the part of the Housing Department, a number of other people ought to have been aware that the woman lived in a state of neglect and needed help.

The coalman came every week to deliver fuel for her one fire. She relied on him for seven days' supply at a time, but that week he had not called and the old woman was without warmth. This is one of the biggest winter dangers for old people. Their pension allows them only a week's supply at a time and if the coalman fails to come there is a risk of death from cold. There was a man who brought firewood, who also called regularly. Both came into the flat to be paid; it was their habit to knock and walk in through the unlocked door. The postman delivered gas and electricity bills during Christmas week and, as for the rent-collector, the ragged curtains and dirty windows were there for him to see. Men from the gas and electricity boards called at regular intervals to read the meters and to do so they had to go through the filthy living-room into the miserable kitchen. During the morning of 1 January a workman employed by Sheffield Public Works Department called to mend a broken firegrate. He told the old woman not to light a fire – even if she had had fuel to do so – until he returned with a replacement. He came back in the afternoon while we were there and he seemed neither unduly surprised nor upset by the condition of the flat. He told us he had seen other old people in similar circumstances, but he did concede 'It's a bit bad.' Nor had he orders to report such conditions to his superiors. An official of the Public Works Department, when later confronted with this, went even further: 'That's no concern of ours. The Housing Department have their own inspectors. We carry out the work and that's all we have to do,' he said.

All such regular callers have an opportunity to see the conditions under which an old person lives, to note the deterioration and to contribute to identifying cases of need. The question is raised whether informing the welfare services is eroding the personal liberty or independence of an old person. But it seems to me that a report, leading to a friendly, investigatory call from a welfare officer or health visitor, is hardly likely to cause serious offence, even if help is refused. It seems far more likely that with the proper approach a person in need will accept the help of welfare services, though 'difficult' cases are recorded. But people are loath to be thought interfering and, if only for this reason and excluding indifference, it is not surprising that those who, because of their work, have access to an old person's home do not report such cases when they encounter them. Often, of course, they do not know how or where to report them. The old woman herself had refused help in the past both from the welfare services and from her neighbours. Only at the last minute, when her condition was desperate, did she accept that she should go into a residential home.

Sheffield's Health and Welfare Department was doubly aware of her case. Her first contact with the welfare services was in December 1968 when a health visitor called because she had been told the old woman lived in dirty home conditions.

At that time the health visitor's report said the flat was neglected but that the old woman was still active for her age and refused a home help and meals on wheels. The health visitor left a card so that the old woman could make contact if she needed help at any time in the future.

Late in 1969 a letter from a woman who visited an old man living in the next-door flat told the Social Care Department that the old woman needed help but that there was no urgency because she was being visited by her son every week. A welfare officer called twice on 22 December but the old woman was out, and again on 29 December. On that occasion the old woman refused to go into a home on either a permanent or a temporary basis, but said she would be willing to have a home help and meals on wheels. The dirt and neglect of the flat was noted and that she was not particularly well cared for. The welfare officer also visited again on 31 December and again on the morning of 1 January, even though she was on holiday, to see if the old woman had decided to enter an old folk's home.

At the request of the welfare worker the health visitor, a state registered nurse with special training in social work, visited again on 31 December 1969. According to her report, later made public by the Medical Officer of Health, she found the flat 'in an appallingly dirty state' cold and without coal or food. She made a fire and a hot drink, both with difficulty because the firegrate was broken and there was no equipment in the flat for preparing food except a pan and an old mug. She reported the broken firegrate to the Public Works Department.

There are several points to be made about the Health and Welfare Department's involvement. Firstly, after the visit of December 1968, when signs of neglect were noted, would it not have been better to mark a date in a visiting diary for three months or six months ahead? To me it seems unlikely that an old person becoming senile would make use of the card the health visitor left. Secondly, a wasteful separation of duties between welfare worker and health visitor is clearly demonstrated. The health visitor is the one who recommends home help and meals on wheels, but the welfare worker is the one concerned with admission to an old folk's home. In such a case one or the other could easily make all the recommendations. Thirdly, the welfare worker was obviously concerned, so much so that a visit was made on her day off, 1 January.

But, despite all these visits, despite the welfare worker's concern, no emergency arrangements were made to care for the old woman until she could be removed to an old folk's home. According to the Medical Officer of Health and the Chief Social Welfare Officer, the earliest date, had the old woman agreed, was 2 January. Normal procedure was being followed; bureaucracy finds it hard to cut corners and procedure takes precedence. But in such cases the care of an old person who is at risk demands procedures which can chop through red tape and provide emergency help.

Immediate action was clearly necessary. On the afternoon of 1 January, just after visiting the old woman's flat, the editor of *The Star* telephoned Alderman Sir Ron Ironmonger, leader of the City Council, who called out the holiday emergency service of the Social Care Department. Alderman Sir Ron also broke off family celebrations to visit the flat (his knighthood had been announced that morning in the New Year's Honours List), and was as shocked by what he saw as we had been.

Admittedly, the old woman's continuing refusals to go into a home made the task of the Health and Welfare Department more difficult, but, as *The Star* was to suggest in a leader following attempts to defend the Department's position, there was a suspicion that 'case-hardening' had taken place. That comment crystallized the criticism of the social services in their treatment of the case. It said:

After all the official explanations it remains a hard fact that Mrs – was left in her squalid Corporation flat without food she was able to eat, without heat or even fuel on a bitterly cold day and in a thoroughly deplorable personal state.

The authorities, in their letters and statements, have yet to tell us why no emergency arrangements were made to care for her until such time as she could be admitted to a home. The reason they have yet to tell us is plainly that no adequate arrangements were made.

At the time, in the circumstances of the case, such a comment was unanswerable, and, indeed, no satisfactory answer was ever given.

Having dealt with the local authority's involvement we come to what Alderman Lambert called the 'paramount' responsibility, that of the family.

The old woman had been a widow for thirty-six years and had lived at the tenement block for thirteen years. Previously, she had lived for twenty years at one of the old districts of terraced houses in Sheffield. She complained that she had been lonely at the tenement and that her present neighbours were not as friendly as those at her former home – although they had tried to help her and been refused. She also said she had fallen several times and hurt herself but had not seen a doctor because she did not want to bother anyone.

Considering the condition of herself and her home, we were astonished when she told us she had a son and daughter-in-law living in another part of Sheffield. The son visited her every Thursday, the day she drew her pension. They arrived later on the afternoon of 1 January and agreed that it would be better if she were admitted to an old folk's home. The welfare officer who had arranged her emergency admission to the old folk's home shortly before questioned them about why they had let the old woman get into such a condition without letting anyone know.

The son said he had thought everything would be all right. Over a year before his mother had told him the buildings would be coming down and he thought it would not be necessary to contact anybody about the conditions. He said that for two years he had made weekly visits to see her and that each time his wife had 'tried to tidy up the place'. His last visit had been six days before.

He added that two years before his mother had had a fall and spent some time in hospital. When she came out she lived with him and his wife for a time. 'While she was with us she did not qualify for an additional pension (Supplementary Benefits) which she had been receiving before. For this reason, and because she is independent, she moved back.' He had asked her if she would go into a home but she had flatly refused. He thought it would be better for his mother 'to go into a place where she would be well looked after', but he did not go to the local authority to see if they could do anything.

Obviously she had preferred to remain independent until the last and her dirty and unkempt appearance would cause people to shrink from her, adding to her isolation. However, despite the independence which her son attributed to her and which she demonstrated in her dealings with the local authority, more could have been done to help her at a much earlier stage. There is no reason to doubt that the son did visit her weekly, but how he could have continued to do so, seeing her condition and the condition of her home every time, without taking action, was in our view surprising.

Four

'Resources are Strained
to the Limit'

In studying a problem which involves the whole community one of the advantages possessed by a newspaper is its ready access to public opinion. The issue of *The Star*, dominated by the dreadful picture of the old woman, which publicized her case, provoked a widespread reaction from the public. The newspaper received its heaviest ever mail and civic leaders were prompted to make public statements, and take action, over an unavoidable issue.

The reaction was indicative of the division within the community and, again, of the ignorance of the problems of the elderly and of the role of the social services. To some people 'they' – blind authority – were to blame; to others the newspaper itself was to blame for disturbing their complacency with shocking facts. It was not what they wished to read in a local newspaper and it was in bad taste. Accusations that washing society's dirty linen in public and claims that such reporting was sensational, gutter journalism, were read somewhat sadly. But apart from those which merely demonstrated an obsessive objection to the role of the press, one could read into others an underlying theme of 'don't want to know'. A significant proportion of the mail showed this reluctance to face up to the situation, a refusal to accept that a widespread problem existed.

Other letters adopted a very unsympathetic attitude to old women in similar circumstances in the city, even going so far as to suggest that the aged who neglect themselves should be left to die. Typical of the more moderate views was the following:

My gran is eighty years of age and she's been a widow for nearly twenty-two years, but not once has she allowed her home to get dirty or untidy. She gets the same pension as anyone else so therefore only allows herself the things she can afford. Yet after your campaign on old folk I read of old people just sitting back and letting everything get top side of them. If every old folk did this we'd be in a sorry state. It's just unnecessary. I'm sorry but they just don't get my sympathy.

In a similar vein:

My indignation, however, was not on behalf of Mrs –, but on behalf of the thousands of old people in the city who, although often in failing health, keep themselves clean and respectable, care for their homes and do not let them become 'foul-smelling' and their curtains 'ragged and filthy'.

Not for these old people the offers of free holidays, the instant place in a comfortable old people's home, the gifts of clothing. They just plod on.

Others were eager to point out that their aged parents or grandparents were clean, good housekeepers and had never had any help from the social services. Why should the dirty, the ones who neglected themselves, be given help?

This was perhaps the commonest criticism of the campaign to improve the lot of Sheffield's elderly and, of course, it does not admit that some people age differently from others. These letters usually pointed out that the writers regularly visited their aged parents and implied a considerable degree of social communication with their elderly relatives. They accepted filial responsibility as a normal part of their lives and had obviously not considered the possible effects if their aged parents had been deprived of their affection. And, whether through ignorance or prejudice, they did not accept that while some old people remain active and alert of mind until an advanced age, others of lesser age, for whatever reason, physical or mental, can become quite incapable of seeing to their own needs. 'Self-neglect' was continually argued, and a point of view was discovered which flatly refused to accept the argument that self-neglect must have some root cause. 'Their own damned fault and they don't deserve help,' was how it was once explained to me.

Others put the relatives' side of the question:

Only someone who takes in an aged relative knows anything about this subject. The way many old people bully and bite the hand that feeds them never gets any publicity. It seems to work in proportion. For example the more secure and comfortable they are then the more miserable they are. The better off financially they are, the more miserable they become, etc.

These are the reasons why they are left on their own so often. Even so there are probably more old people living comfortably with their young relatives than there are old people on their own. These young people will never get those years back, neither will they be thanked by anyone. They are often sneered at by the old people they help, and they usually resolve never to do it again at any price. Aged people need qualified help and money should be provided for this.

Another correspondent who signed the letter 'A Terrible Relation' wrote:

The relatives are the first target – but as with everything else there are two sides to every question. Those who point an accusing finger would perhaps like to hear an inside view.

Wardens and helpers make fires for these old folk. Then, because it's too much trouble to put fuel on, even though it's by their feet, they just let the fire go out and wait until someone else comes to relight it.

Washing to be done three times weekly, bedding and personal clothing – worse than a baby's washing through incontinence and loose bowels. This, in spite of protective clothing being bought, but 'can't be bothered' to wear. Still insists on being taken out, though now having great difficulty in walking.

After a lifetime of struggling to get a decent home together and bringing up a family, the relations are not so keen on having it ruined by someone who has lost the will either to live or to keep clean. Wet, smelly car seats, chairs and carpets are no joke either to the person concerned or the relatives, but the former seems oblivious to any chaos caused. To come to this after a lifetime of fastidiousness bordering on the unnatural is too disheartening for words.

This relative – an only one – is after ten years of varying degrees of illness and hospitalization just as weary as the person concerned, who, incidentally, apart from recent falls indoors, has suffered nothing worse than a cold in all the nearly eighty-four years. How I dread getting old.

The last two letters define problems faced by relatives who care for the aged and show good reason why sons and daughters are reluctant to take on the burden of poorly and cantankerous old people, although the first writer is over-concerned that the elderly are not duly grateful for what is done for them. This attitude of 'you get no thanks for it' was widely expressed and, it would seem, is a valid reason why previously willing people gradually withdraw their help. The need to feel appreciated is obviously important and there were people who said that after criticism of the Social Care Department, as a result of the case, its professional workers were extremely disheartened. Initially even the professionals might have been upset by exposure of the frailties of a service limited by manpower and expenditure, but the newspaper made it clear what those limitations were and pointed out that it was not its intention to 'pillory the social services'. Indeed as dozens of problem cases were reported to the paper a good working relationship was quickly established between the journalists and the local authority services.

Some of the harshest criticism of the social services came from the medical profession and its validity cannot be discounted.

One lengthy letter from a doctor is worth reproducing in its entirety. He claimed that the case was by no means an isolated instance and advised careful inspection of the 'excuses' of the welfare departments.

For the past year I have requested these departments to take care of a woman who became too feeble to live alone after being discharged from Lodge Moor Hospital. Virtually nothing was done apart from the odd visit when the usual platitudes were muttered and she eventually became bed-ridden, and, but for good neighbours, would have rotted. Several phone calls to Social Care produced nothing tangible and finally I was informed that as she was now bed-ridden she was suited only to a geriatric hospital. A phone call to the hospital resulted in a visit – two weeks later – by their staff and finally a letter which said she would be taken to out-patients for a more full examination to see what measures would help her to stay at home. About four days after I received this, and two or three days before Christmas she died – alone.

Another case concerned an old man who was senile. He was found wandering in the rain clad in shirt and trousers. He was found two or three times, once by me, in a gas-filled house – he didn't know the gas was on. He was totally disorientated, defecated where he sat and I found him one day gnawing on an uncut loaf.

Frequent telephone calls to Social Care were met with hard luck stories about accommodation difficulties until one day I informed them that in the event of his death I would accept no responsibility and would inform the Coroner that Social Care were aware of his circumstances. Behold a place was found for him.

I can quote many more cases over the last two years, but what of the present? One old lady in her eighties has become crippled by a collapsed spine, is registered blind – partially sighted – and has chronic bronchitis. She is dependent upon the home help. On Monday December 22 she told me that the home help was to be discontinued for Christmas until the following Monday. I pointed out to the home help that she was a special case – in a perfect world she would be in hospital – and that if any special considerations were going, she needed them. The home help communicated with her supervisor and the result? No home help until the following Monday. Who went and mended her fire on Christmas Day? – Me.

The politicians and their Welfare State make me sick. We pay lip service to an ideal and pass the buck.

While I cannot publicize my name for professional reasons I am quite willing to show this case to your reporters.

We did in fact see the old woman and confirmed what the doctor said. She lived alone, left her door open so visitors could admit themselves, was very nearly bed-ridden – perhaps as near as makes no difference – and one can think of few situations more dangerous than an 80-year-old partially blind cripple trying to boil a kettle of water on an open fire, as she was forced to do.

Another doctor added bitterly:

I was impressed when Sir Ron Ironmonger managed to arrange the admission of Mrs – into a Social Care Home. The five hours she had to wait compares very favourably with the many months my equally deserving patients had had to wait and are still waiting for a similar admission. Perhaps Sir Ron Ironmonger would let me know his contacts as I too would like my patients to jump the queue.

A statement by Dr Patrick Lambie, the British Medical Association's spokesman in Sheffield, confirmed the family doctors' opinions on the shortage of places in old folk's homes.

'Sheffield really deserves the title of a geriatric slum,' he said. 'The provision for old people in the whole of the Sheffield Hospital Region* and in Sheffield city in particular, is appalling, mainly because of lack of money, lack of planning and adequate foresight over the past years.'

His view was that the shortage of old folk's homes blocked the care of the elderly in two ways. Firstly, in their own homes because a tremendous strain was thrown on home helps, district nurses and meals on wheels. 'Many old people are not ill in the medical sense but too old to look after themselves. The place for them is in a hostel, but Sheffield has lagged way behind the rest of the country in the provision of this.'

When old people recovered after hospital treatment they were often in need of hostel accommodation which did not exist. They were either sent home – too old properly to care for themselves – or kept in hospital.

And in hospital they are blocking beds for people at home who are ill. The result is that we cannot get people who are sick into hospital for medical care, nor can they be adequately cared for in their own homes because home service resources are strained to the limit. The social services and home helps work very, very hard, but there are not enough of them. These old people are left mouldering in poky

*Presumably called the 'Sheffield' region because its board meetings and headquarters are in Sheffield. In fact it stretches from Leicester in the south and across Lincolnshire to the Wash, as well as including Nottingham, Derby, Lincoln, Chesterfield and the area around Sheffield. When one sees it on a map one wonders whether the person who drew its boundaries was asked to produce the most unwieldy administrative area he could imagine.

little flats, they are frozen when they cannot pay their fuel bills, often they cannot light their own fire and there is no one to look after them.

I and other doctors like me have had patients on the list for old people's accommodation for months and months, sometimes years, and we cannot get them the place they deserve. The doctors have been complaining about this situation for a very long time but we have met with very little success.

The doctors' grievances, particularly about the lack of residential homes for their patients, are real and understandable, and as we will see later this was a very considerable grievance. One can envisage the frustration of a conscientious family doctor when the local authority says his patient is fit only for a geriatric bed in hospital, but the hospital returns responsibility to the local authority by saying it will examine the patient to see what measures will enable him to be kept at home. There may have been no hope, either in a residential home or in geriatric care, for the first patient the doctor spoke of. Even so, have we any excuse for not making the last years, or months, of fading life as comfortable as possible?

Nor should family doctors, with many calls on their time, have to perform what are properly the duties of health visitor, social-care worker or even those of home helps in ensuring that old people living at home and alone are being properly cared for. It is, however, traditional for a doctor to pay regular visits to the old and enfeebled within his practice and such calls must be of comfort to the elderly even when there is little the doctor can do, in a strictly medical sense, for those whose only real ailment is advanced age. But such calls are valuable as a check on the health and welfare of an old person, and, unfortunately, with the changes now taking place in family doctoring, they could become less frequent, due to the pressure of work on doctors and the need to reorganize their services on a more efficient basis.

In an earlier interview Dr Lambie explained these pressures on Sheffield's family doctors, each of whom has an average of 2,500 patients. On a fairly normal day he could expect up to a hundred patients at his two surgeries, morning and evening. To give five minutes to each would have meant about eight hours a day in surgery work alone and to find time for administrative work and calls on patients in their homes he had to beat what he called the 'three-minute barrier' in his surgery. So the trend is towards group practices and appointments for patients rather than waiting-room queues, and Dr Lambie expressed the view that far too much of a doctor's time was taken up with home visiting, much of which he said was completely unnecessary. He thought it would be much better to examine patients in a properly equipped consulting room and, with proper grouping of doctors, it ought to be possible to have an ambulance service to bring to consultations those people who could not get about very well. He felt, however, that people should not be cut off from skilled medical attention in their own homes and, with proper grouping of doctors and the attachment to those groups of a district nurse or health visitor, a more comprehensive service to people who, through sickness or senility, needed care at home could be achieved.

The idea of a health team of doctors, nurses, local authority services and administrative staff working together in a community is already in operation in some parts of the country and a report of the Ministry of Health in 1967 said: 'Such a team is ideally placed to provide personal medical services, including preventative, to the population it serves.'

Dr Lambie pointed out that for some years Sheffield's general practitioners had been trying to get a degree of attachment of local health and welfare services to general practice. This becomes important in the light of a hospital turnover rate which is higher than ever before: as a result more post-hospital care falls on these services. In these circumstances it seems wasteful and illogical that a family doctor and a district nurse or even a home help can have little or no contact when jointly caring for a patient newly released from hospital. A number of health centres are planned in Sheffield and, if the degree of participation the doctors want is given, improved contacts at a community level ought to provide better services for the elderly. It seems to me that the greater the degree of decentralization of services, the better those services will be for the community they serve.

The care of the elderly newly released from hospital to their own homes has in a number of instances shown that liaison between hospital and local authority domiciliary services is not all that it should be. Cases came to light of elderly people being left alone and helpless because Sheffield's home-help service had not been informed of the discharge. In one of them a fifty-nine-year-old man who had suffered a fractured femur was alone in his flat for forty-eight hours, a case which led Miss J. Parker, Sheffield's Home-Help Organizer, to complain of a 'definite weakness in the link between hospitals and the Home-Help Service'.

The unification and strengthening of local authority social services and the appointment of Directors of Social Services under the Local Authority Social Services Act, 1970, ought to lead to improved contact and liaison between doctors, district nurses, hospitals and domiciliary services and perhaps make the way clearer for community health centres to be established. But family doctors, jealous of their position as independent contractors to, and not employees of, the National Health Service, might have to sacrifice some of their traditional independence in the process.

The criticisms made of Sheffield's welfare services as a result of the case and the doctors' comments on the lack of residential homes in the city brought a factual reply from Alderman Mrs Patience Sheard, Chairman of the Health and Welfare Committee. Her letter to the press outlined Sheffield's services for the elderly as they existed in January 1970, together with estimates of current expenditure.

She welcomed an attempt to focus on the needs of the elderly and added: 'My only regret is that this was not done sooner since I myself have repeatedly and publicly in the City Council stressed the necessity for the steady and uninterrupted expansion of all our services for the old.'

Her figures showed that Sheffield 'already' had 20 social-care homes, providing 740 places plus 37 short-stay beds, which would cost the city £517,000 in 1970. A further home would be handed over soon and another completed in August, adding 94 new places. Another with 44 places was scheduled for completion in 1970; builders would commence work on another and the Corporation was expecting tenders for a further home, the two adding 90 places.

£307,000 was being spent on the wages of the equivalent of 490 full-time home helps and 38 wardens, although 826 women were employed, part-time work making up the service. Meals on wheels served 121,021 meals. Health visitors paid 13,483 visits to people aged over 65; there were 158 nursing and auxiliary staff employed in the home-nursing service and a further 43 in the night-attendant service. A special service had also been provided for the incontinent at a cost for the next year of £10,000.

Mrs Sheard commented: 'Certainly we need many more old people's hostels than these, but it would be a catastrophe if the general public were to be lulled into the belief that this most challenging problem could be solved simply by the provision of more old people's homes.'

Mrs Sheard also pointed to the fact that some of those most in need refused practical help; that there was difficulty in recruiting staff, and that demands on the services grew year by year. Sheffield was spending well over £2,000,000 that year on services to the elderly.

She ended: 'If there is a simple answer, and I doubt that there is, it can be put this way – a society that has a conscience must be prepared to pay a greater share of its personal income to help its ageing members – remembering that one day they too will be old.'

Naturally enough, Mrs Sheard stressed the positive side of Sheffield's work for the elderly. From the Labour Party's point of view there were at the time sound political reasons for emphasizing the extent of its provision for the old, but Mrs Sheard must be credited for not belittling the problem and saying quite bluntly that if social services were to be improved at a local level the ratepayers would have to be prepared to foot the bill.

The negative side of the picture came when a 'leak' to the press gave the author a copy of a report to the Health and Welfare Committee from the Social Care Department, dated 14 October 1969, which said that the Social Care Department was 'no longer providing an effective service'. It was not surprising that this report, which asked for the appointment of five additional welfare officers and one welfare assistant at a cost to the city of about £6,000 a year, was not made public until 7 January. It made no bones about the shortcomings of the service which staff shortages and increasing work had caused.

Increased staff were asked for on five grounds: (1) High caseloads. (2) Approximately two hundred referrals each month. (3) Impossibility of adequate follow-up work with residents (those in social-care homes), applicants awaiting places in social-care homes and others. (4) Increased number of homes since area system was formed on 1 June 1967. (5) Additional holiday cases from 240 to over 1,000 a year.

The report said the area system consisted of all referrals being allocated to one of five areas appropriate to their geographic location and that each area had at present one area social-welfare officer, one social-welfare officer and one welfare assistant, with the exception of one area which had two social-welfare officers because it included boundary extensions from Sheffield into Derbyshire.

The report said:

Since the adaption of this method of dealing with clients, the work has increased considerably and the Department now has an average of two hundred new referrals each month, approximately three fifths of whom are elderly with problems of residential care and other family problems, the other two fifths being general family casework and problems of homelessness. With this continuing influx of new cases, many of which are long term, the average case-load per worker has increased to 160 clients and in addition each worker has some responsibility for approximately eighty further persons in residential care.

It will be realized that intensive casework is not necessarily needed nor would in any way be possible with these numbers of clients but the situation has now been reached where only superficial work can be achieved with the majority of clients and *an effective service is not now being provided*.* This situation prevails because frequent urgent inquiries and emergencies take precedence as they arise over follow-up work with existing or prospective residents as well as other families or individuals in difficulty.

In addition the Department has recently extended its service with regard to short stay and holiday relief.... It is expected that approximately 1,000 clients may now use this service during the year as compared with previous figures of 240 per year, and this volume of additional work will throw increased strain upon the area staff.

Also, since June 1967 three further Homes have been completed with two more to be available during this present financial year. This again provides additional work for area staffs so far as visiting and liaison with matrons is concerned.

It is most necessary for the standard of service to be adequately maintained that an increase in the establishment be made ...

(It was also learned at that time that the waiting list for admission to old folk's homes had grown to 1,079, of which 363 were classified as being in immediate need.)

Even allowing for the temperate language of the Town Hall, that is a startling report of the kind which calls for immediate action. Sheffield's Personnel Services Sub-Committee delayed acting upon it at its November and December meetings, and when a question was asked at the January meeting of the City Council, it was explained that the delay was due to the nearness of the 1970–71 estimates and the need to establish priorities. However, when the Personnel Services Sub-Committee met on 22 January, it doubled the requested number of five new officers and increased the establishment by ten, thus fulfilling a budget pledge by the Finance Chairman Alderman Isidore Lewis, that people would be given priority in his allocations.

Emergency action was also taken to increase Sheffield's provision of old people's homes. On 13 January, at the request of

Author's italics.

Mrs Sheard, the Town Clerk wrote to the Department of Health and Social Security requesting the building of four old folk's homes for the next three years, doubling the normal rate of building at that time.

These two acts can obviously not be separated from the criticisms which had been made and from the intensive public debate which was still going on.

It would be unfair to criticize councillors and officials for not being aware of problems until they were pointed out. What that public debate did initiate was a change of priorities, and the Social Care Department, which a Conservative councillor described as 'the Cinderella of the Corporation', gained much wider recognition as a vital public service.

Similarly, Sheffield had not asked to increase its building loan sanctions for old folk's homes above two a year because of the difficulty of getting Department of Health and Social Security permission for even that meagre number. It is worth recalling that when Mr Richard Crossman visited Sheffield in September 1968, shortly before becoming social services head, he criticized Sheffield's lack of planning in the provision of accommodation for old people, only to be given a flea in his ear when Sheffield informed him that his new ministry had vetoed the city's plans to build two new homes a year. The city was told that financial circumstances would only permit one new home a year. But in November Sheffield put two new homes a year back in its estimates, which were allowed.

It was against this kind of financial background that Sheffield made plans to build old folk's homes and, obviously, part of that planning had to be an assessment of the likelihood of loan sanction being granted. It was therefore a bold and unequivocal step when Mrs Sheard demanded that Whitehall permit the programme to be doubled on 13 January 1970.

It was, however, the right time to make such a demand. At a national level, with an eye to the huge Conservative lead in the Gallup polls and a reminder that Sheffield was one of its few major strongholds in the provinces, the Labour Government could not ignore criticism of its provisions for old people. Nor could it forget that Sheffield's Tories would strongly challenge Labour for control of the City Council in May.

The result was that when Dr John Dunwoody, Under-Secretary at the Department of Health and Social Security, toured the Sheffield region early in April he announced an 'exceptional allocation' for building old people's homes in Sheffield – ten in three years instead of the twelve asked for. He said at the time that the four hundred new places which would be provided in three years would bring Sheffield up to the national average for residential homes for the aged, but as we shall see later this was a questionable assertion. Whether the national average itself has any meaning or is anything like good enough is an entirely different matter, but for Sheffield, at least, any increase in this building programme was a step forward.

As well as criticism, these two valuable acts by the local authority, and a rush of troublesome cases to the newspaper, there were also constructive suggestions for coping with Sheffield's problems from both private individuals and Sheffield's politicians.

It is well worth while looking at some of the suggestions put forward in January 1970, considering their usefulness and seeing whether they were acted upon to a significant degree. But it is enough at this stage to say there was a touch of prophecy in a letter which said: 'I wonder how many of those who are now loud in their condemnation of the old people's plight will spare them a thought in twelve months' time?'

One of the first suggestions was that voluntary and statutory work should be coordinated on a district basis. Alderman Sir Ron Ironmonger said Sheffield had considerable voluntary resources, but these should be coordinated for greater efficiency to avoid overlapping of aid and to make sure no needy cases were overlooked. Voluntary workers should be organized on a district basis and the first step should be a visiting programme. Sir Ron said he envisaged a coordinating committee of the City Council and voluntary interests – not a committee of the Council as such, but one which would report its work to the Council.

He said that he was determined that the battle against loneliness and neglect should not be a seven-day wonder but a continuing effort and he added that he hoped the scheme would get off the ground as quickly as possible. 'We are talking in terms of days rather than weeks,' he said.

This proposal, which could have laid the foundations for the wider involvement of the community in the care of the elderly, did not get off the ground. It was officially felt that to call public meetings of all interested bodies would delay giving elderly people the aid that they needed and that the establishment of a central committee was inappropriate at the time.

But virtually nothing took the place of Sir Ron's proposal and one felt at the time that public meetings between professional and voluntary social workers and interested members of the public could have led to a wide interchange of ideas and perhaps led voluntary bodies to new objectives in the care of the elderly. Looking back, my view is that Sheffield missed a valuable opportunity. District organizations could have been the keystone in identifying the needy cases, providing community care and calling in the professional services when they were needed. Also, some form of central organization, even though its formation was less urgent than putting workers into the field, could have helped. Certainly there was room at some stage for a committee of laymen, experts, councillors and representatives of voluntary bodies, which could have pooled its knowledge, assessed its abilities, examined its priorities and laid solid foundations for the future.

The Corporation did appoint a liaison officer to coordinate the work of voluntary and statutory services, but he was to meet a depressing degree of indifference from voluntary organizations. Nine months later Sheffield had little or nothing new in the way of district organizations and little more coordination between voluntary bodies and between them and the statutory services than had existed before. What comes into question is the very existence of the voluntary resources Sir Ron mentioned, and, where they do exist in recognized organizations, their ability to expand their activities and maintain the continuity of service which must be given if their efforts are to be successful. There is no doubt that lip-service is paid to what people always refer to as 'the extremely valuable' contribution of voluntary bodies when, in reality, their work is often restricted in its aims, prejudiced towards certain groups and classes of people and short-sighted in its outlook.

What the Corporation failed to do was to give the lead, as Alderman Ironmonger suggested, in creating district organizations at a time when the people of Sheffield had a newly heightened awareness of the problem in their midst. Such organizations have been successfully set up in other towns, even down to street-warden level.

Another useful suggestion which was not acted on came from the Conservative Group on the City Council. They proposed that the Corporation should set up a permanent investigation team to seek out cases of need, the work of which would be governed by an all-purpose committee, which would be responsible for enlisting the aid of all who could help. A permanent team of 'troubleshooters' had considerable potential.

There was also a call for the churches in Sheffield to combine in order to visit old, lonely and depressed people. Again, this was a matter which was talked about, but not acted upon promptly.

The reaction continued into February when some very fine-sounding words came from the Labour Group's meeting on 2 February. It appeared that urgent action would soon be taken. 'Just as we have a universal system for the education of children, so we ought to have a comprehensive system of service for the elderly,' said Mrs Sheard, after the meeting. 'I am proposing now that the council should pledge itself to finance and implement an overall plan for the development of all services for the elderly to such a level that each retired person will have the right to decide for himself the manner in which he wishes to live.'

Labour's plans fell into two stages – 'remedial' and 'long-term'. The remedial action would be taken by the Health and Welfare Committee's Welfare of the Elderly Sub-Committee which would review its functions to strengthen formal links with the Housing Department at committee level; consider the practicability of establishing a single point of referral for all elderly persons in need; and nominate a specific officer with overall responsibility for liaison with voluntary organizations through the establishment of direct and formal links between voluntary workers and groups of health and welfare officers practising on a district basis. Long-term action would follow a survey in depth of the needs of the old and how they should be tackled by the Corporation's new research and intelligence unit.

Alderman Mrs Sheard said:

I am full of new hope that we are at the beginning in Sheffield of a new era in regard to the life which our elderly citizens will be able to live. The really urgent need in Sheffield today is to have a detailed and thorough assessment under the auspices of the research and intelligence unit in the Town Clerk's Department of the size of all services required, bearing in mind the amount of help available from relatives and voluntary workers to provide a comprehensive service. This will be a mammoth task which has never been done before in any part of England at this comprehensive level and it will take some time. The council must be prepared to implement the final plan, certainly in financial terms, to the extent, of course, that professional workers become available over a period.

In the end one thing is certain. However much we extend the statutory services, however many professional workers we employ, nothing can remove from the hearts and minds of the old the bleakness of loneliness and desolation except the feeling of belonging to a community which cares for them and respects them for all they represent.

How long does it take to consider the practicability of a single point to which old people can take their troubles? This is an absolute essential, but eleven months later Sheffield was still waiting. To my mind excuses that the city was waiting for a new Director of Social Services are irrelevant. It could have been decided and acted upon in a matter of weeks. Mrs Sheard warned that a thorough survey would take some time, but how much? At the time the plan was announced Sheffield, in fact, did not have a research and intelligence unit as such – only one man had been appointed. Eight months later a preliminary report, which would say how the research and intelligence unit intended to tackle the survey, which would then say what the needs of the elderly were and how they should be dealt with was still awaited.

On 17 February Sheffield announced a record fifteen per cent rise of £441,000 in its Health and Welfare Budget, bringing total expenditure for the financial year 1970–71 up to £3,359,154. For the elderly, Mrs Sheard announced 'the maximum provision possible consistent with the difficulties of recruiting staff'.

The home-nursing budget would increase by £37,117, bringing its total cost to £223,000, giving an increase in nursing staff with the emphasis on the night service. The cost of the home-help and home-warden services would increase by £70,000 to £430,000 with the employment of fifty-five additional home helps and twenty-four home wardens, as well as an area organizer. The cost of paying ten new social care officers would be included in the £97,000 increase in spending on residential care.

Despite the criticisms I have made, the demand for doubling the building rate of old folk's homes, the increased budget and the improvement in establishment of social-care officers, home helps and home wardens showed that Sheffield City Council were prepared to take positive steps to ease the plight of the elderly people in the city and that, within financial limitations, services for the aged would be improved.

One must comment, however, that all the action taken continued to concentrate measures for caring for old folk in the hands of the Health and Welfare Department. There was not enough devolution of interest to include the store of enthusiasm which had been aroused in the city and, at a time when the climate of opinion was right, an opportunity of laying foundations for bringing care of the elderly down to a local community level was lost.

Five

Some Problems of Old Age

Some of the problems of the elderly can be serious and complex, demanding time, effort and money. Others are, on the surface, simple in character and yet irksome to resolve. Citing the difficulties facing Sheffield's Health and Welfare Department, Alderman Mrs Sheard gave the example of a social worker who had made ten visits to one old woman in an attempt to persuade her to take a bath – all without success. Such a case illustrates the time, work and expense which must go into the provision of welfare services, often to achieve little or nothing. On the other hand, some old people's worries can be relieved merely by advising them which agency of the State or local authority, or which voluntary organization, can help them.

Physical disability, mental infirmity, loneliness, poverty and inadequate housing are headings which state the major problems of old people, but many of these factors are frequently present in the same case and they become interwoven so that clear-cut definitions cannot be drawn. Being crippled and housebound causes loneliness and isolation from the active world outside and the loneliness can lead to the mental decline of the old person concerned. Comparatively slight physical disability can be aggravated by inadequate housing, making care a more demanding task, while the shame of poverty can have a similar isolating effect, cutting the elderly off from the activity of the more affluent society outside their homes.

Physical disability, loneliness and extreme age are often combined. '... Aged eighty, lives alone in one room, crippled by arthritis and has not been out for three years,' records the case file. Or '... Aged eighty, alone and crippled, cannot walk or dress herself. . . . Aged eighty, totally blind in one eye, partially blind in the other, crippled by rheumatism and arthritis, sleeps in chair, has no relatives in Sheffield . . .'

And when extreme age is involved the children on whom the old people rely can be elderly, or pensioners themselves. One case concerned a couple aged ninety-five and ninety. The daughter on whom they relied and was herself sixty-seven, had fallen ill and was unable to care for them. Another couple were both eighty-four, the husband ill and the wife senile. Their daughter, aged over sixty, had a sick husband to look after as well. In another case a disabled couple aged seventy-nine and seventy-two had their shopping and housework done by a younger sister, aged sixty-four, who was now finding the work beyond her. A further case demonstrated the shortage of places in hospital ; a family doctor was unable to arrange the admission of an old woman who lived alone and who was almost blind and subject to blackouts and falls. She needed sheltered care because of the increasing demands of an invalid husband on her diabetic daughter.

Such cases add force to the argument of the Seebohm Report that when old people come under the wing of the Social Service Department support should be given to the whole family.

Sometimes such support seems to be reluctantly given. An old man aged eighty-one, living alone, had fallen into a serious state of self-neglect and had built up a stubborn resistance to outside help. Although still alert and active he refused to accept that he was now an old man ; he had continued to work as a clerk until the age of seventy-eight. He was seen surrounded by the filth of his home, shaking with cold on a January morning but refused permission for a fire to be lit. His electricity was cut off and he would not use his coin gas meter, probably because it was in his cellar and without electric light he could not see his way down the steps.

A widower since 1965, he had been visited regularly three times a week by a married daughter, but the strain of caring for him had led her to the verge of a nervous breakdown ; she had been advised by her doctor to stop her visits for the sake of her own health and the old man had been without her help for a year. The daughter complained that when she contacted the local authority welfare department they did not seem to want to know about the problem and said her father's welfare was her responsibility. Her husband contacted the department again and it was agreed that a health visitor would see him. The health visitor had been seeing the old man for a year and repeatedly asking him to accept help. Each time he had refused. Finally he did agree to accept the assistance of a home help, much to his daughter's relief. The situation had been a great burden to her and she had been afraid that people would think she had abandoned her father.

Unlike many old people who live in a state of neglect this old man was not mentally befuddled and perhaps he had come to realize the distress he was causing his daughter. 'I appreciate these people are willing to help me,' he said of the social services, 'but I have turned them down for so long because I am by nature an independent man.'

A visit to him a month later, after his home had been cleaned and was being kept tidy by twice weekly visits from a home help, saw a remarkable change. He was clean, cheerful and seemed to have taken on a new lease of life. His neighbours had always helped him and now seemed happier to do so. He was no longer living in the kitchen and his only remaining problem was solved when the gas board moved his meter from the cellar to the ground floor.

In the case of another old man the impression was given that his sons had abdicated any responsibility for him. He lived in an even worse state of neglect, dirty, bearded, clothing shiny with grime. His house was thick with dust and dirt and, typically, he too lived in the back kitchen, where rubbish and decaying scraps of food littered the table top. He walked badly, with the aid of a stick, and for this reason did not venture into the dark yard to the outside toilet. As a result there were stinking buckets under the table from which he ate. He too was a widower and neighbours, who gave him a hot meal each day (but understandably shrank from the unenviable job of cleaning his home), said his decline had started with the death of his wife.

He was known to Sheffield's welfare services. A woman who collected his coal money had telephoned the Social Care Department, but he had refused help. The Public Health Department had also called to examine the house because it was in a clearance area. Neighbours were bitterly critical of his sons, who lived in the city, for not trying to help the old man. He could not remember the last time he saw them and none of them had visited him at Christmas 1969. Yet he was inordinately proud of them for having 'got on'. He himself had been a skilled workman. We found him friendly and cheerful towards visitors and grateful for their company because he rarely stirred from his one room. When out in bad weather he had fallen and injured himself on a number of occasions and he showed recent deep wounds in his leg where he had fallen in the street. This was a case which made us wonder how hard the welfare services tried to persuade some people to accept help. We knew from the neighbours that he had previously refused help and yet, after braving the stench of his kitchen for a while, persuading him that it wouldn't be a bad thing if he had someone to clean for him was a relatively simple task.

Friendly persuasion was the solution in both these cases, but both epitomized the level to which an old person can sink and the conditions which can end with a cold, squalid and lonely death. But other old people, who often have clean homes, regular food and no mental deterioration, can have problems which become too much for them to bear alone.

One such case was an old couple who battled against adversity in the most trying circumstances. The husband was eighty-eight, almost helpless because of arthritis in his hands and legs and house-bound for three years. His wife was seventy-six and had had to look after him as though he were an infant for eleven years. It meant day and night nursing for her. She had to feed her husband, shave him, wash him, dress him and undress him. Each morning she was up at six to light the fire and her sleep was disturbed because her husband was racked with pain and tossed and turned all night. This situation was leading to a deterioration in her own health, although she was assisted by a home help. During May 1969 she had been fortunate. At her doctor's insistence her husband had been taken into the geriatric unit of a Sheffield hospital for a month to give her a break.

This was a couple remarkable for their determination and dedication to carry on. The old woman was grateful for the month she had been free from the worry of her husband and felt that she had been fortunate to have such relief. But she was also of the opinion that 'the authorities' should provide more rest homes where people like her husband could go to give relatives a holiday.

Seebohm points out:

Families looking after old or handicapped members can be helped to carry the burden, not only by the provision of good domiciliary services, but also in the knowledge that short-stay accommodation can be provided to meet emergencies or to allow the family respite or a holiday.

At the beginning of 1970 Sheffield had only thirty-seven short-stay beds in residential homes for old people; quite clearly that provision is not enough for the numbers who would want to take advantage of short-stay beds to give temporary relief from the worry of the kind of intensive care which the previously quoted case shows is often given. To the old woman in question it would have been of enormous relief if she could have been guaranteed a place for her husband on a regular basis. The task of family doctors would also be made easier in the knowledge that short-stay beds are readily available.

Arthritis is the ailment which cripples more old people than any other, yet hospital provision for its treatment is sadly lacking. The Arthritis and Rheumatism Council presented a report in May 1970 which showed that in the whole of the Sheffield Hospital Region only fifty-six beds were available for sufferers from rheumatic complaints – one bed to every 56,000 people. Yet it is the medical opinion of the Council that early treatment will help to arrest arthritis before it reaches the chronic and crippling stage.

Loneliness, even in the most modern developments, is frequently encountered and can be debilitating and demoralizing for an old person. All too often old people die alone and their bodies remain undiscovered for days, sometimes weeks, and no one can say how they suffered before death brought release or whether their lives could have been saved if they had been able to call help. At Sheffield's giant flat development at Park Hill, the badly decomposed body of an elderly man was discovered on 9 January and none of his neighbours, or shopkeepers nearby, remembered seeing him since before Christmas. His neighbours hardly knew him, and the caretaker said he had often had to break into flats to reach sick old people or the bodies of those who had died.

Another case concerned an old woman who lived in a group of about eighty pensioners' flats and newspaper deliveries behind her door dated the time of her death at a week before she was discovered.

The Sheffield and District Coroner, Dr Herbert Pilling, said lonely deaths such as these occurred about once a month and reports throughout 1970 confirmed this figure. Exposure of this problem brought fresh demands for the installation of alarm systems in old people's flats and requests for improved warden services in places where large numbers of people's dwellings were grouped together.

In comparison to extreme neglect, severe disability and the strain it throws on partners and relatives, and the constant tragedy of loneliness, many of the problems of old people appear trivial to younger and active people but can still cause worry and distress to the elderly. Imagine a situation where an old woman stands on her doorstep asking passers-by if they will come into her home and feed the gas-meter for her. It is not money she wants, but assistance. The old woman is only five feet tall and the meter is seven feet from the ground. She has twice fallen when trying to climb up on a chair. She has mentioned her difficulties to the collector but her problem does not seem to have reached anyone in authority at the gas board. Others like her have to ask strangers into their homes to go down steep cellar stairs to feed their meters. These are simple problems, and easily solved when drawn to the attention of gas and electricity boards, but inconvenient and distressing for the old people who have to live with them.

Sometimes, in preference to moving a badly sited meter, the gas and electricity boards offer to change them to quarterly accounting. This, however, can present other problems and a quarterly account is a lot of money to pay out all at once for someone with no more than the old age pension on which to live. Sometimes coin meters are used as a form of saving when the collector presents a cash rebate.

The change to a quarterly electricity account brought a peculiar, and it seems to me extremely irritating, problem for one seventy-six-year-old woman. At the last collection from her coin meter she expected her usual cash rebate. Instead she was told it would be deducted from her first quarterly account and the electricity board seemed reluctant to part with the money immediately. I dealt with the matter personally and was given an edifying example of how dehumanized bureaucracy can make an old person feel it is remote and indifferent to the needs of its customers. It seemed that to give the old woman the cash rebate she wanted would upset a computerized accounting system and to find out how much rebate was due would mean a print-out from a computer in Leeds. Such print-out information could not be telephoned to Sheffield, I was told. The question 'Why not?' produced some totally unsatisfactory blather about procedure and eventually the electricity board office agreed to telephone for the information and make the money available for the old woman to collect. This was not good enough. Why should a none too active old woman have to travel to the city centre from the outskirts to collect money which was owed to her? I finally extracted a promise that the money due would be posted within the next few days.

This may seem to the reader a small matter over which to make such a fuss – after all the money would have been deducted from her first quarterly account. But in this case she had used the rebate as a form of cash saving to pay her coal bills and without it she would have had the worry of an unpaid coal bill and perhaps have even put the continuity of her coal supply in jeopardy.

It was particularly distressing to find pensioners whose gas and electricity had been cut off because of unpaid bills. One old man was living in the winter by candlelight, eking out his pension and supplementary benefits to pay off an outstanding £15 bill at £1 a week. Out of a total income of £7 6s. a week he paid £2 rent, £1 for coal, £2 10s. for food and a few shillings for radio batteries and bird-seed for his two budgerigars – his only company. He explained that his bill had become too high for him to pay because he had been unable to obtain coal and had had to keep his electric fire on. At that time he had coal but no electricity and the only room he could afford to keep warm in the depths of winter was his living-room, where he had taken to sleeping on the couch.

The cost of keeping warm is a never-ending dilemma and a fearsome worry for pensioners. They find the cost of coal hard enough to meet – a bag a week is sometimes all they can afford – and deliveries can be uncertain. We recorded one case of an old woman who had been without solid fuel all winter, and many others found it difficult to get supplies. Smokeless zones have forced old people to pay for dearer smokeless fuels and the cost of this fuel, apart from its shortage, is an increasing burden on an inadequate pension.

With the rises in gas and electricity charges which have been forecast, the likelihood is that more and more pensioners will be unable to pay their bills. Moving into modern centrally heated flats – except where a Corporation makes a standard charge for central heating – does not help their financial position and they can be faced with the tragic choice of eating or keeping warm. At the Liberal Party Conference in September 1970, Alderman Wallace Lawler of Birmingham estimated that about 60,000 old people had died from cold the previous winter. It seems generally accepted that numbers of this order are at risk in winter.

Like gas and electricity, the Post Office is a public service and on many occasions it was found that pensioners lived in blocks of flats without a nearby telephone. Demands for handy telephones were frequently made. It was discovered, for example, that at the giant new Kelvin block, with over three hundred flats for old people and where emergency calls to doctors often need to be made, there were no public telephone boxes; this was a year after the first tenants moved in. The community association had raised the matter only to be told by the Post Office that it was reluctant to install public boxes because of vandalism in blocks. The Post Office is only prepared to install telephone boxes in profitable positions and does not take social need into account. A box for a block of old persons' flats is not a money-making proposition and so it is left to organizations such as Sheffield's Council of Social Service to pay for one to be installed in a flat whose occupiers make the telephone available for other tenants. This can only be done where people are prepared to tolerate the inconvenience of others coming into their home and when the charity has funds available to pay for the telephone.

While gas and electricity boards and the Post Office seek to make profits they are also monopolies which provide vital social services. Old people have no alternative but to accept rising gas and electricity prices and the social obligations of these power suppliers will increase as more and more old people's flats are built to standards which demand central heating. Unless – and how unlikely it seems – the Government is prepared to raise pensions to a level which removes the increasing worry of paying for gas and electricity, then it must consider ordering the boards to give concessionary rates to pensioners. Similarly the Post Office ought to be required to provide the necesary service of a telephone to groups of old people's flats. There should be no difficulty in designing a lock-up box to which only the old people concerned have keys. In my view it is scandalous that the provision of such a vital, often life-saving, service has to be paid for by charity.

Old people who need help and know they need help are sometimes baffled when they turn to the authorities and if bureaucracy shunts a needy person from department to department he will more than likely give up trying. Housing departments have welfare officers, health and welfare departments have social-care officers, district nurses, health visitors, night-nursing services, incontinency services, chiropody services, mental-health services, home wardens and home helps. Both local authorities and the Department of Health and Social Security provide aids for the disabled. There is the Supplementary Benefits Commission and a large number of charitable and voluntary organizations who can give help to an old person.

If each town and city had one central point where needy people could take their troubles, discuss them with experts and be directed to a suitable service, whether voluntary or statutory, then a great deal of time and trouble would be saved. With the Local Authority Social Services Act now in force, and with the unification of local authority welfare services, such centres should be easier to establish. I believe that the main reason why well over a thousand cases were brought to the notice of *The Star* during 1970 was because the newspaper was not representative of established bureaucracy and people expected that we could find a quicker way through the rocky channels of officialdom. Many others, whose cases were not recorded, telephoned for advice because they did not know where else to ask.

Many old people would never ask. They endure hunger, cold and poverty, too proud to complain, fighting infirmity and loneliness – the problem that statutory social welfare services cannot solve. So frequently are old people alone, not just for days but for weeks, that they can lose touch with reality and their solitary existence crushes the spirit and the will to live. But not in every case. Loneliness should not be confused with proud and stubborn independence. Compared to some of the tragedies of solitary neglect, the case of an eighty-nine-year-old Boer War veteran held a touch of humour. His stubbornness forced Sheffield Corporation to conduct a two-year campaign of persuasion to get him to move from his decrepit, run-down house, which stood alone in a slum clearance area where everything else had been levelled. For the sake of his own health and welfare he needed a better home than the damp house with boarded-up windows where he lived in one room. But for two years he re-fused to speak to council officials and finally when he did agree to move his pride was still unshaken. 'I'm not being evicted. I'm moving because I want to move,' he said. Foolish pride, per-haps, but understandable and, in its own way, admirable. As he explained at one stage, he kept pigeons and they provided one good reason for not moving: 'My birds wouldn't know where to fly home.'

Six

Thirteen Steps to
Make a Prison

The Seebohm Report summarizes everything which is wrong with housing for the elderly in this country.

We have no hesitation in placing good accommodation, both housing and homes, high on our list of priorities for old people, for we regard them as keys to the successful provision of other kinds of service. For instance, the home-care services are bound to be over-extended unless the right kinds of accommodation are provided in adequate amounts, in the right proportions and in the right places ... we must stress here that not only are the numbers of dwellings provided for the old by local authorities quite inadequate, even at the present rate at which they have been built over the last two or three years, but that far too little attention has been paid to the encouragement of housing associations to share this task.

Housing is a contentious political issue. But even politicians find it hard to argue against fact. The fact is that enough new houses have not been built since the war. Indeed, the Labour Government's failure to keep a pledge to build 500,000 new homes a year by 1969 may be seen in the future as one of the major causes of their 1970 election defeat.

There is no doubt in my mind that had such a target been reached by the previous Conservative Government, and maintained throughout Labour's six years of office, Britain's housing problem would still be some way from seeing a solution, for I well remember attending conferences of the National Housing and Town Planning Council nine and ten years ago when experts were speaking then of the immediate need to build half a million new houses a year if the country's housing needs were to be met.

It seems that only now, through the activities of organizations like Shelter and shock tactics such as television's *Cathy Come Home*, is the country as a whole becoming properly aware of one of the most urgent social needs of our times. It is sad to recall that the magical figure of half a million was the target set by Labour's 1966 Election Manifesto, *Time for Decision*, and that Mr Harold Wilson pledged it would be reached in 1969. The nearest the country has got to this total was in 1968 when, according to Ministry of Housing and Local Government statistics, 425,835 houses were built; but in 1969, target year, house building slumped badly to 378,325. Over all, however, Labour's six years of power showed a better average house-building rate than that of the previous Conservative Government. In the years 1960–64 an average of 322,393 houses were built each year, while between 1965 and 1969 the average was 401,372.

The very need for Shelter and the heart-rending stories of families split up and living in local-authority hostels are grim commentary in themselves. For the elderly, the work of bodies like Help the Aged, and other charities which build old folk's homes, appear to have taken on a new impetus, recognizing a need which statutory services are not fulfilling.

One reason for the failure of Britain's post-war housing policy becomes apparent when one looks at the proportion of our national wealth we have spent on housing in comparison with the other industrially advanced nations of Western Europe. Over the years we have spent considerably less of our gross national product on housing than our European neighbours. Although by 1967 the United Kingdom's expenditure on housing had risen to 3·7 per cent of our gross national product, Belgium spent 5·0, France 6·2, Italy 6·1, Netherland 5·7, Sweden 6·4 and West Germany 5·2 per cent. When expressed as buildings completed per thousand inhabitants the 1968 figures show that France completed 8·5 homes per thousand, Italy 6·3, Netherlands 9·7, Sweden 12·7,* West Germany 8·4, while the United Kingdom figure was 7·7. Earlier years show equally

*1967 figures

disproportionate figures to the United Kingdom's disadvantage. This clearly demonstrates that in comparison to other countries we have not devoted enough of our national energy and wealth into housing and rehousing the fifty-odd million people of this country and that, if that elusive figure of 500,000 houses a year is ever to be reached, we must spend more.

Sheffield, however, has contributed a greater than average share to new house building in this country since the war. It has built about 40,000 houses in the past twenty-five years and incurred enormous debts in doing so. In the 1969 financial year 2,724 new homes were completed, bringing the total of Corporation-owned dwellings to 71,610. At the same time, the amount spent on providing and improving Corporation houses in Sheffield rose to a staggering total of £121,761,695, of which £105,983,946 represented outstanding loans.

At the moment of writing, Sheffield was building more than a quarter of the houses under construction in the West Riding of Yorkshire, 2,205 at the end of June 1970, out of 8,226 for the whole county. Leeds had 1,586 under construction. Sheffield's completions for the first half of 1970 were 1,173 against 940 for Leeds. For projects on work which was yet to start Sheffield had approved tenders for 1,593, out of 4,064 for the whole county, of which Leeds claimed 835.

But despite this enormous effort and expenditure Sheffield is still faced with housing problems which will take years to resolve and it must urgently improve a situation which offers little comfort to its thousands of elderly people who need to be rehoused, the very people who through age and circumstances are most dependent on social housing to put a decent roof over their heads.

A case taken from files shows a great deal of what is wrong with housing for the elderly in Sheffield and epitomizes the endless wait some old people have to endure before they can be suitably rehoused :

... The niece says the elder sister, aged eighty-one, has been in poor health for a number of years, in and out of hospital with bladder trouble. The younger, aged seventy-four, takes care of her as best she can, but she too is now feeling her age and finding it increasingly difficult. Their home is owned by a private landlord and the niece says they have been on the Corporation's waiting list for an old person's dwelling for sixteen years.

Both are now having to live downstairs. The elder sister cannot climb the stairs, nor can she get outside to the toilet and has to use a commode. They have been frequently visited by Corporation officials because the niece has continually tried to get something done for them. Last week they were offered a Corporation flat – an upper flat – which they knew would be no use. Apparently this was the best the Corporation could do and because they had to refuse it the younger sister was in tears when she telephoned the niece to tell her what had happened ...

The factual situation of housing the elderly in Sheffield is clearly illustrated in a series of answers to written questions which Sheffield's Housing Manager, Mr M. J. Aldhous, gave early in 1970. His replies were frank and to the point, but revealed a lamentable shortage of houses for the aged when compared to the numbers awaiting rehousing, and showed that the design of flats for old people left a great deal to be desired. In fact, one could go so far as to say that much of the new housing which Sheffield Corporation has listed as 'purpose-built' for the aged shows little or no appreciation of the needs of the aged and is downright badly designed. These are harsh criticisms to make of highly praised developments and mammoth flat blocks which have won architectural design awards, but they need to be said.

Certainly, it was astonishing to learn from Mr Aldhous that half of Sheffield's 'purpose-built' dwellings for the aged contain flights of stairs which must be negotiated when entering or leaving. What did not surprise was that these flights of stairs were a barrier which turned the flats into cells for many of the cripples, arthritics and heart cases who live in them.

In the past Sheffield's most prestigious development, the Park Hill–Hyde Park complex of gigantic flat blooks, has been criticized for its 'penitentiary' style of architecture, but investigation revealed that it and Kelvin, a similar much newer monster in another part of Sheffield, really were prisons for many old folk. These three enormous blocks contain over 1,000 flats 'purpose-built' for the elderly and yet every one of them has a flight of stairs which must be climbed to reach the door. Instead of locks and bars, thirteen steps are the prison.

As well as these three blocks Sheffield has about 2,700 upper flats for the old in two- and three-storey blocks which are approached by staircases, and in all over 3,350 of Sheffield's 7,350 'purpose-built' flats for the elderly have staircases, giving rise to constant complaints.

Nearly all old people's flats are one-bedroomed with a living room, kitchen, bathroom and WC, or a bedsittingroom with kitchen, bathroom and WC. Sheffield also has 2,450 of these one-bedroomed flats for childless couples or single persons not of pensionable age. It was not known how many of these were occupied by elderly people but presumably many were, and of them 1,650 were approached by staircases.

Old people need special fittings and when descriptions such as purpose-built are used one thinks in terms of non-slip floors, power-points at waist height, easily accessible fixtures, non-slip baths, etc. But all Sheffield provided was handles to assist getting in and out of baths and this compares badly with what other local authorities were able to provide for the old.

However, in Sheffield, the most worrying aspect of all is the waiting list for old people's dwellings. At the beginning of 1970 about 9,500 old people – more than the present stock of accommodation – were awaiting rehousing by the Corporation. Of these 7,961 lived in private houses and 1,414 were Corporation tenants. Apart from slum clearance, which should mean immediate rehousing, the wait for a bedsittingroom flat was five years, for a one-bedroomed upper flat ten years and for a one-bedroomed lower flat an interminable sixteen years. A total of 474 old people were on the medical priority list for rehousing and their wait could be anything from a few weeks to nine years, according to the availability of the accommodation requested.

During the financial year 1969–70 Sheffield was building seven hundred more old folk's flats and two hundred one-bedroomed flats for persons not of pensionable age, and since 1965 the over-all proportion of one-bedroomed dwellings in new Corporation housing was forty-five per cent, of which more than two thirds was let to pensioners.

This pressing shortage creates many problems in Sheffield and has a significant effect on slum clearance, even though this has priority. A number of cases were recorded where elderly people were the last to leave derelict streets because flats were not available in the districts in which they wanted to live.

One example concerned an eighty-seven-year-old woman, who by February 1970, had lived alone on a derelict street for a month. Because of damp in her bedrooms she had taken to sleeping downstairs on a couch in front of the fire. Her isolation frightened her and she was terrified at night. She had been told by the Housing Department the previous summer that it would not be long before she was in a new home, but in December a letter from the Housing Manager told her he was unable to predict when she would be rehoused. It depended on dwellings becoming available for re-letting in the area she wanted, over which he had no control. The old woman, quite spry and active for her age, was helped by a daughter who lived near her condemned home. Ideally, she would best have been rehoused in a block of old people's flats not a hundred yards away. But none was available there. In this case a local councillor did all he could to speed her rehousing and arranged for police patrolmen to check the area at night to assuage her fears. He commented : 'It seems the problem has been that she has been limiting herself to this area where her daughter lives.'

How unfortunate it is that this is a problem. In such a case, with a pensioner aged eighty-seven, it makes no sense to rehouse her away from a helpful daughter. If this happens, and it frequently does, helping an old person involves travelling and becomes a time-consuming matter. The result is that another case might be added to the bulky files of the Social Care Department.

The Housing Department begins seeking a suitable vacancy or re-let for such elderly people even before notice of entry is served – in this case it was September 1969 – but the old woman was not rehoused satisfactorily until the end of May 1970.

We do not know how long before September 1969 the Housing Department began its attempts to find this old woman a new flat, but it took nearly a year, even with slum-clearance priority, to rehouse her. Nor was it a case where there were bureaucratic slip-ups or where the matter was pigeon-holed and forgotten. The Housing Manager himself was in close touch and the local councillor constantly pressed the matter with the Department.

We saw another example of a slum-clearance rehousing problem when we visited a court of twelve houses in a clearance area. Only four were still occupied, three by elderly couples. One of these couples, because of the wife's serious illness, had been on the medical priority list for rehousing for four years. All the houses were damp, with crumbling plaster, and no longer in a sound state of repair. The lavatories were outside in the yard. The couple on medical priority had made repeated requests for rehousing in a particular district. This was in order to be near a daughter who gave them a great deal of assistance, but nothing had come of their requests. Another couple in the court were younger pensioners, the husband aged only sixty-seven; the chimney of an empty house next door had fallen through their roof. Between July 1969 and January 1970 they had received only one offer of a flat from the Housing Department and that a bedsitter in the giant Kelvin Development. They did not want to move to Kelvin in any case, nor did they want a bedsitter which they considered far too cramped for an active couple.

Ironically, another old woman in the same court aged seventy wanted a bedsitter in Kelvin so she would remain near her daughter. She had been offered a flat on an estate some distance away. The paucity of offers, which are often not what is desired, illustrates that because of the shortage there is very little housing choice for the elderly in Sheffield. Often, it would appear, old people have to take what they regard as an unsuitable offer, because there is nothing else for them.

The situation also suggests that insufficient investigation goes into the rehousing of an old person, or that when investigation does take place it is very often too late. In theory, people being rehoused are given three choices, or more precisely two refusals. But in practice, because of the shortage, the extent of choice is limited. It is common practice for the Housing Department to make offers they think might be suitable outside the specified area of choice. When there is little or no chance of a vacancy in the area of choice they have no alternative but to do this.

What appears to be needed is deeper and earlier investigation into the rehousing needs of an old person long before demolition, or even for that matter notice of entry, is due, to try to suit their needs to the availability or likely availability of dwellings. Housing Departments like Sheffield's will argue that a great deal of this is already done, but constant complaints and a high incidence of cases like those described tell a different story.

On the subject of prior investigation, we must talk about Kelvin, the newest of Sheffield's three giant blocks. At Park Hill, Hyde Park and Kelvin a considerable number of elderly cripples were discovered to be to a large extent imprisoned by the thirteen steps down to their flats. Park Hill, with 996 homes – 296 for old people – was completed in 1960 and Hyde Park, with 1,169 flats and 373 for the elderly, followed. It could be argued that residents' disabilities developed during their tenancy but no such argument could be made for Kelvin, where residents started moving into the 947 flats and maisonettes in April 1969. One third of these flats are for the elderly and investigation showed that old people crippled by arthritis and other ailments were among those moving in. At the end of February 1970 officials of the Kelvin Community Association estimated that at least forty of the 270 pensioners already in residence were permanently trapped there because of the steps, and that for a great many others the steps constituted a serious obstacle.

During a visit to these flats I saw an old man of over seventy, who was in no way crippled but already, after only a week's tenancy, was finding the stairs a problem and because of them excused himself from seeing me to the door as I left. On another visit I saw a ninety-two-year-old woman, crippled by incipient gangrene in her feet, who lived with an eighty-five-year-old sister. She had been out of the flat only once in nine months. The community association had provided her with a wheelchair so that she could be pushed about the flat and with a level entrance she could have been wheeled out of doors. Not surprisingly the couple wished to move and they were under the impression that a transfer had been granted, but, unfortunately for them, all they had received was a Housing Department receipt of their request for transfer.

The situation at Kelvin would have been a great deal worse for the old people there but for the unstinting work of the community association, which had formed a volunteer team of housewives. They checked on every old person moving in, discovered his needs and then took on the tasks of visiting, cleaning and shopping. One city councillor, annoyed at the press publicity on the situation, claimed, in contradiction to the Housing Manager and the Housing Chairman, that the flats were not necessarily for the elderly but were for single people. Even if her claim had had any validity the fact was that the flats were occupied by pensioners, and very often not those at the younger, more active end of the old-age spectrum. For example, in ten days in January 1970 fourteen old people, all aged over eighty, were moved in. It was still worse to learn that one old woman of ninety was moved into a Kelvin flat too ill to sign her tenancy agreement.

Kelvin was fortunate in having such a public-spirited community association, but even its members were finding their work a strain because of the large number of old people and the degree of incapacity among them, and although their work was encouraged by a toiling resident welfare officer they felt they did not receive enough help from the Corporation. The association was critical of the Corporation for failing to established proper community services at the time when people began to occupy the monolithic block.

One example was the lack of a community hall, which was planned for completion in April 1970 and then deferred until

September. This resulted in problems over the use of an unoccupied flat as a morning meeting-place for the elderly and as a place where local clergymen could hold services for those unable to travel to church. After some wrangling the use of a flat was granted for a nominal rent, but ironically it was of the thirteen-step variety.

The situation at Kelvin, Hyde Park and Park Hill revealed a deplorable state of affairs. Deplorable because old people who were obviously unsuited to the thirteen-step flats were being moved into accommodation they should never have been offered in the first place. But beggars can't be choosers. The three huge blocks provided between them over a thousand flats for old people, a very considerable addition to Sheffield's inadequate stock of housing for the elderly, and more suitable flats were not available.

We must also consider the position of the younger, active pensioners who move into such flats, remembering that they will grow old in them and, as likely as not, begin to suffer from the confining ailments of old age. The time comes when they need a ground-level flat, or at least one in which climbing stairs is not obligatory.

Alderman Harold Lambert, Sheffield's Housing Chairman, gave an answer of a kind to this question at a meeting of the City Council in June 1969. 'Obviously if a tenant is infirm and needs a level entrance other accommodation would have to be found,' he said. It is perhaps of some significance that his answer was in reply to a question about the staircases at Kelvin, where elderly cripples were being moved in many months later.

But where are such one-level flats? What chances are there for such a move when Sheffield's waiting-lists stretch for so long? In particular, how can the move from an upper flat to a lower, ground-floor flat be arranged when the time spent on the waiting-list is 16 years? Any solution of a transfer to a lower flat completely disregards the upsets an elderly person will suffer from moving home. Obviously it is far better to rehouse old people in accommodation which will be suitable for them for the rest of their lives.

It was not just in Park Hill, Hyde Park and Kelvin that staircases were a problem. Similarly cases were discovered of old people confined to the upper floors of two- and three-storey blocks. Indeed, in one area of Sheffield, pensioners were found living in bedsittingroom flats from where they had to climb down ninety steps to reach the shops. These bedsitters were at the bottom of a block of maisonettes built on a steep hillside and the old people complained of the stairway to the shops, the remoteness of the flats and the lack of services. Sheffield's City architect, Mr Bernard Warren, described them as 'obviously not suitable' for old people and said they had never been built specifically for the elderly. Nevertheless, here was an example of old people living in single-person accommodation.

No humane housing management can refuse a tenancy if it is requested and the dwelling is available to let, but I am sure that housing officials would be far happier in their work if they had much more of the right kind of accommodation to offer and therefore could be in a position to point out that, for the old, certain properties have disadvantages. At the moment the Housing Manager's job is to attempt the impossible, to fit a quart into a pint pot.

Similarly, the chairmanship of the Housing Committee is a political 'bed of nails', a most unenviable job of trying to maintain and increase building rates and maintain standards at a time of constantly rising prices and interest charges. Criticisms of housing policies, and therefore of the housing chairman, come thick and fast (not least from journalists like myself), while praise is hard won.

Alderman Lambert at least has the satisfaction of knowing he can defend a housing record better than most in this country, and his defence of the design of Park Hill, Hyde Park and Kelvin has a solid foundation. The reason for them having the much-criticized thirteen steps is because they are built on what is called the 'deck access' principle. This gives three floors between long, wide balconies, which have been called streets in the sky. A feature of the design is that old people's flats are the top of the three levels between decks and are entered by going down from the deck above, whereas for the two-floor family maisonettes below them there is a level entrance from the deck beneath. This design gives more space for light and air between decks, providing much needed high-density housing in a comparatively small acreage near the city centre, leads to a great deal of prefabrication of services and saves money.

Alderman Lambert said the mid-air streets compensated people for the loss of a home at ground level and helped to retain the neighbourliness of the old terraced streets. He also said they gave first-class opportunities for social intercourse, but this assertion is open to argument. However, steps apart, the flats and maisonettes in the three giant blocks are pleasant and attractive living units and the old people do enjoy the warmth of the central heating system.

But it is all too easy to say that flats with stairs are 'ideal' for old people who are active and can negotiate them. This is to ignore the fact that the shortage of level-entrance and ground-floor flats condemns cripples and other handicapped people to live in flats with access stairways.

Any argument that the problems of the elderly, especially with staircases, were not fully appreciated at the time when Park Hill and Hyde Park were planned is only half-way acceptable. After all, the pre-war and early post-war building of old people's bungalows in many parts of the country show that the avoidance of stairs was a design consideration, and the need to cut out stairs is obvious to anyone who gives the problem a moment's thought.

It is no argument at all when applied to Kelvin, which came much later and when such problems must have been appreciated. Conservative opposition councillors claimed that Kelvin should not, and need not, have been built, and that it was out of date before work started on it. Cancelling it, they pointed out, would have presented no difficulties because it was constructed by the Corporation's Public Works Department and not by a private contractor. However, Conservative criticism of anything involving the Public Works Department is suspect because of their ideological opposition to the use of a provenly efficient Public Works Department on large contracts.

Even so, my view is that insufficient sociological consideration was given to the planning of these giant blocks, and this view was vindicated when, after press criticism, some plans for new deck-access flats were sent back to the Sheffield City Architect for redesigning in order to eliminate the steps.

Sheffield has more problems than most places in building the ground-level and level-entrance accommodation that old people need. It is a very hilly city and suitable sites are not readily available. But some of the estates and developments which the Corporation has built since the war show an imaginative approach to making the best use of these hillsides, not least of which are the monolithic flat blocks at Park Hill and Hyde Park. In building for the elderly, however, the approach has been completely without this imagination.

Undoubtedly the city has sought to achieve a balance of ages in the new communities its redevelopment has created, but the contention has to be made that its old people's housing, especially that at Park Hill, Hyde Park and Kelvin, was dictated by expediency. Perhaps the problems which this type of development creates for the elderly were not readily understood by the political decision-makers, but on the other hand it may well have been the expediency of providing cheap, high-density housing which was the overriding consideration. Sheffield's topography prevents the building of all one-bedroomed accommodation for the old at ground level, but one can also contend that a more imaginative architectural view could well have produced more old people's flats with a level entrance.

But the biggest limiting factor in producing the right housing for the old is money. I have already mentioned Sheffield's massive housing debt of almost £106,000,000, and the qualification for Government subsidy weighs heavily with local authority planners, architects and quantity surveyors when new building is under consideration. The reason why Sheffield constructed the two- and three-storey blocks (with entrance staircases to upper flats) was to keep within the Ministry of Housing and

Local Government cost yardstick and standards, and thus qualify for subsidy, and it was easier to keep within the yardstick if three-storey blocks were built.

If costs are kept to within ten per cent of this yardstick, subsidy is given on capital cost. But if costs are even 11 per cent over, then even loan sanction is refused. According to the experts, general building costs tend to rise so swiftly that they outstrip the upward adjustment of Ministry allowances and there are times when these are a year out of date on costs.

Furthermore, a local authority's housing finance problems do not decrease with the number of new houses it builds. The financial problem can become worse because it is increasingly difficult to let Corporation houses at rents which reflect the cost of building (e.g. £3,250 in Sheffield for a three-bedroomed house) and the cost of repaying loans. For profitable house-letting, local authorities rely on older council properties which were built when costs were smaller and interest rates lower. These, in fact, subsidize the rents of newer, more costly houses, and so, as the stock of new, high-cost high-interest houses becomes bigger than the stock of older houses, another financial problem has to be faced.

It was claimed that Sheffield was building too many new council houses, which eventually would force up rents. New building would have nothing but a detrimental effect on present rent levels and it was doubted whether the 2,000-plus new homes the Corporation built every year were necessary. This, of course, was the Conservative opposition view on the City Council, which said the Corporation should concentrate on building for the old and the handicapped and encourage a great degree of owner occupation even among those being moved from slum-clearance areas. Although there should be no slow-down of slum clearance they argued that greater emphasis should be placed on improvement rather than demolition of new houses. But in the past few years Sheffield has approved over 10,000 discretionary grants for the improvement of old houses at a cost of roughly £1,250,000, so obviously improvement of older properties is running at a high level.

There is something to be said for the Conservative opposition view, especially when it demands greater concentration on building for the old. But at the same time we must remember that young families have an equal right to be considered, especially in a city where rented accommodation on the free market is extremely difficult to obtain, even for those earning sufficient to pay dearly for it.

All the same, we are left with a situation which Sheffield must somehow improve both in quantity and quality if the housing problems of its old folk are even to approach any sort of satisfactory solution in the next decade. This brings us to the question of whether Sheffield has devoted the right proportion of its housing effort to the needs of old age in the past. In the financial year 1968–9 Sheffield completed about 2,200 homes, of which thirty-nine per cent were for the elderly, and building rose to 2,700, completions in 1969–70 – a creditable total at a time when house-building slumped nationally. Since 1965 Sheffield has aimed to build forty-five per cent of its new housing as one-bedroomed accommodation and the city's ruling politicians argue that this is the right balance between building for families and the elderly and taking into account the needs of slum clearance.

Sheffield aims to clear 2,400 slum houses a year and at the last count 21,132 old houses were included in future programmes for investigation to decide their fitness for habitation. This is not to say that all these houses will be found unfit, but some of them, even if they are fit, might have to be demolished under comprehensive redevelopment schemes. It is generally agreed that with the present slums and with the deterioration of other, older properties not as yet investigated or scheduled, Sheffield has about 20,000 slum houses to be cleared. The deterioration of property has kept this figure fairly steady at the 20,000 mark for a number of years despite the fact that 24,000 slum dwellings have already been demolished.

Politicians in power in Sheffield argue that in this situation to devote forty-five per cent of building expenditure to one-bedroomed accommodation, mostly for elderly people, is the right proportion. As Sir Ron Ironmonger stressed in a Council debate, the Corporation also had to honour its obligations to people on the general waiting list and those in slum clearance areas, as well as to the elderly. There were not enough houses for any of these categories and they could not solve the problems of one category to the detriment of another.

More up-to-date figures than those previously quoted, from October 1970, showed a general waiting-list of 10,889, an aged persons list of 7,262, a single persons list of 1,146 and a supplementary list of 1,174. On these figures forty-five per cent one-bedroomed flats for new building seems a balanced figure, but there is an extra factor. As Mr Aldhous pointed out in January 1,414 of the old people on that list were in Corporation houses, waiting for smaller flats. Many instances have been found of old couples, even widows and widowers, living in two- and three-bedroomed houses from which they wished to move because their homes had become too big for them. Rehousing them in flats for the old would free these family houses for occupation from the general waiting-list. If, even for a comparatively short time, the percentage of building for the old were to be increased, it might free some of these houses for the general waiting list.

There is a drawback to this suggestion. Those old people awaiting a flat who are already Corporation tenants in family houses have a good roof over their heads. A great many other old people on the list live in slums and their best opportunity for rehousing from decaying and inadequate homes is when a Clearance Order gives them priority. In the present circumstances would it be fair to keep them waiting and take up an increased percentage of dwellings for the old by depopulating family-type houses still occupied by the elderly? It would seem not, and freeing these houses for families, apart from what gradually takes place in the normal course of events, must be seen as a long-term solution.

There is an attitude which demands that housing from the local authority should always be cheap. On one occasion we visited a man and his wife living with two small children in a dreadful, tiny slum house, not because they needed to, but because they had refused a Corporation house because 'the rent was too high'. The father said the rent of the slum was less than £1 a week and he wasn't going to pay four or five pounds for a council house. 'They' could find him something cheaper; why should he bother to look for a new home? It was up to 'Them' to provide him with a cheap home. He refused to state his earnings, perhaps because his wife was present, but said he worked as a furnace-hand in a steelworks – possibly one of the best-paid manual jobs in Sheffield, where take-home pay of over £30 a week is not unusual.

Attitudes like this can only lead to the accusation that in the past councils like Sheffield's have been too paternalistic in their blanket provision of subsidized housing for the community. This contention is supported by the fact that roughly one third of all houses in Sheffield belong to the Corporation and owner-occupiership is over ten per cent below a national average of about fifty per cent. Socialist doctrine professes to abhor any form of selectivity and there are cries of horror at any suggestion of 'means test'. But already a degree of means-testing has crept in through rent-rebate schemes such as the one operated in Sheffield, which, when it was introduced in 1967, was fought to the bitter end by tenants' associations.

The new Conservative Government now intends to force the affluent Council tenant to pay more through a national rents-rebate scheme. If this will lead to more money being available to help the needy who must be rehoused, then there is merit in the Conservative proposals. But, over all, it is the new Government's stated intention to save money on housing subsidies, which must mean that the proportion of gross national product which is going into local authority housing will be reduced. The new Government wishes to encourage more owner-occupiership, itself a commendable aim which should lead to a revival of private house-building. But such a revival will be of no benefit to the elderly who, for financial reasons, must look to the local authority to provide the better standard of homes they so desperately need. At the time of writing we do not know how, if at all, Conservative selectivity will help to house the old.

There is a great deal to be said for selectivity, especially if it will turn the direction of social housing towards providing for the neediest members of the community, the greatest number of whom is the old. The housing needs of the old must have greater priority not only in Sheffield, but throughout the country, to give them bungalows and properly designed flats. Among all categories of people who seek shelter from local authorities the old are the ones who can least afford to help themselves. Their income is small and fixed, constantly reduced in purchasing power, and, unlike the affluent young workers of today, few of them had the opportunity to contribute to good occupational pension schemes to ensure the financial independence of their old age.

All arguments about council housing boil down to questions of social justice. What we must closely scrutinize is the social justice of present-day council housing and decide whether it really is providing for the most needy members of the community – the old, the truly homeless, young families in stringent financial circumstances and those uprooted by slum clearance who are unable to rehouse themselves. Our resources must be more directly channelled towards helping these classes of people and not, as at present, providing a blanket coverage which encompasses those well able to find and pay for their own homes without local authority assistance.

If the old are to be given social justice in housing, we must spend more money and make greater efforts to see that the final years of their lives do not consist of a penurious existence in a damp and cheerless slum. The selfish, so-called affluent, society, owes it to them.

Seven

'Purpose Building'
for Old People

The present shortage of dwellings for the old has a historical basis and can be traced back to the early post-war years. Then Government encouragement led local authorities to build mostly family-type houses. Putting better roofs over the heads of the elderly was, very largely, a secondary consideration.

The imbalance in favour of families is shown by the fact that between 1945 and 1960 only ten per cent of new homes built by local authorities were one-bedroomed, while thirty-eight per cent were three-bedroomed. Between 1962 and 1965 however, greater recognition of the needs of the elderly led local authorities to make twenty-seven per cent of their new housing smaller dwellings for old people, and the percentage has since increased. But, as Seebohm was to remark in 1968, 'Little attempt has been made to estimate the total need for housing for the elderly, but it is clear that need greatly exceeds supply.'

While the political and financial reasons for not building enough houses for the elderly are understandable, if not excusable, it is a sad state of affairs that, after twenty-three years in which housing has been a major part of all political platforms and the subject of innumerable conferences, debates, discussions, investigations and political battles, the most authoritative document produced on social welfare should say the housing needs of the old had yet to be estimated.

In that passage Seebohm was talking about numbers, but what of design and the relationship of old people's housing to the community and social services? Has enough investigation gone into deciding what types of housing are best suited to the old people who will occupy them? Who can say what proportion of old people either rehoused or awaiting rehousing suffer physical handicaps or need regular medical treatment for their ailments? What proportion of the elderly population are helped by families and friends to the extent that their capacity for independent living will be retained well into advanced age without the help of the social services? Considering the failure of a big authority like Sheffield to build sufficient ground-level and one-level accommodation for the old, it is obvious that insufficient investigation has gone into the planning of aged people's dwellings to fit the physical condition of those who will live in them.

After newspaper criticisms of the Kelvin development one Sheffield councillor replied by saying that it was impossible to assess the needs of the elderly tenants until they had moved in. The authority could not know how many old people there would be and how many would need a warden or a home help. In any case, many of them had not received such services while living in old houses owned by private landlords. Why should they need them when they moved into a modern Corporation flat block?

Nonsense of this sort only hurts the image of a local authority and its ruling party. Of course the local authority knew how many old people were moving into the flats for the simple reason that they knew how many old people's flats were contained in the block. How many would need such services as warden and home help ought to be known by prior investigation, but, obviously, in the case of Kelvin it was the move in to Corporation property which brought the problems of old people to the attention of the local authority. Similarly, when a large number of old people are concentrated in one giant flat block, communal needs are highlighted to a far greater degree than when the old folk are scattered throughout the many streets of a slum clearance area. Their needs can be, and should be, investigated before they are moved into new flats, especially when such a move means a complete change of environment and circumstances and when the flats in question are not suitable for old people with physical infirmities.

A great deal of such investigation is needed because, if one thing is plain, it is that the incidence of infirmity among those living in, and moving in to, council dwellings is high. Sheffield of course, keeps a medical priority list and a place on it follows investigation by the Health and Welfare Department. Recommendations by a family doctor do not guarantee that a name will be added to the list and allocation is eventually decided on a priority basis, which is combined with personal choice, by the Housing Special Sub-Committee.

A number of the local authorities around Sheffield stated that they did not keep medical priority lists and their attitude suggested that they felt such lists were meaningless. One did, in fact, use the world 'meaningless'. Another said medical certificates were 'ten a penny'. Instead they decided cases on their merits as they arose, taking the view that keeping a list had no point when nearly every old person could get a doctor to support a request for rehousing on medical grounds. If doctors honestly support requests for rehousing so frequently, this is further proof that the housing of the elderly is worthy of greater consideration on the grounds of design and amenity than it has received in the past.

That old people need special consideration when their housing is designed is so widely accepted as to hardly need reiteration. It would not need repeating and emphasizing if, in the past, local authorities had paid it sufficient attention. But until they have made a thorough investigation, on a local basis, of all the design factors relating to housing the elderly and how these will affect the domiciliary services of health and welfare departments, they will continue to pursue policies which have all the appearance of being haphazard.

Seebohm, for example, commented:

Because of the special requirement in housing for old people (for example in size, fittings and heating), and because it needs to be sited close to shops, public transport and other facilities and in close relationship with housing for other age groups, there is particular urgency for an accurate assessment of needs on a local basis and for this assessment to be kept up to date. What may seem slight changes in the numbers of elderly people in the community may have drastic effects on the demand for housing and other services.

The last sentence in this passage assumes particular importance when we consider not just that we have a population proved to be ageing, but that the largest percentage increase will be among the very old.

Seebohm points out:

In England and Wales there are today about six million people over sixty-five, representing approximately one in eight of the population. A little over a third of these are seventy-five or more. Moreover the registrar general's projections suggest that at least for the next twenty-five years the number in the older age range will grow both relatively and absolutely.

Whereas the population as a whole is estimated to increase between 1971 and 1991 by 17 per cent, the range 65–74 will only increase by 6·8 per cent, but the group over 75 by 35 per cent. Since the major part of the problem of old age is concentrated in this higher age group the implications for the personal social services are obvious.

Obvious too are the implications for housing the elderly. In Sheffield, we have already seen that failure to do the obvious – to build for the old without staircases – has created difficulties. And if similar mistakes are not to be made in future, local authorities must take urgent note that the steepest rise in elderly population will be among the very old. Accordingly, the best possible planning of community services and interior safety fittings must go into future housing developments for old people. Adding them as an afterthought when their need has been proved by occupation is not satisfactory.

But experts in housing and caring for the elderly have, in general terms, long recognized this need for pre-planning. They have defined the problems and suggested good solutions on the basis of the experience. Unfortunately, the politicians have acted too late and too indefinitely at both national and local levels. In this context it would be wrong to think that Seebohm (1968) had anything revolutionary to say on the subject of housing old people. What Seebohm said has been said many times before by many people. The effect of the Seebohm Report was to invest greater recognition and standing in those opinions and to give them a better chance to become the policy of Government.

For example, and especially since investigations in Sheffield are the basis of this book, let us look at what Sheffield's Housing Manager, Mr H. J. Aldhous, said in a paper 'Housing for the Aged' at the annual conference of the East and West Ridings Region of the National Housing and Town Planning Council in May 1964.

The independent housing of old people is important and is becoming increasingly so, especially since the former solution whereby the old lived in with young members of the family is not now so generally accepted either by reason of lack of space or lack of will. The young need to live their own lives in their own way: this does not necessarily conflict with the ways and habits of their parents but 'in-law' trouble is no imagined grievance: it indubitably exists and leads to a very great amount of family conflict.

His paper went on to give a graphic description of the ageing process.

... Arteries harden, mental faculties weaken, joints become arthritic, lungs bronchitic, and the decline into senility throws an ever-increasing burden on the younger elements of the population whether they be family or communal. In the brave new world we may well keep all our faculties at the highest level until late middle age when life may end without a whimper, but we are concerned with the here and now and accommodation that is suitable for the active man who has only just retired creates real difficulties for him fifteen or twenty years later if he lives so long. He is elderly at sixty-five, but active, able and willing to be independent, but as time inexorably goes on he becomes aged and infirm, less mobile and in need of ever-increasing care. He is satisfactorily housed in a self-contained flat at first, but finally needs full-time attention in hospital. From a state of independence he becomes increasingly dependent on others until he is finally completely dependent, increasingly lonely as he outlives friends, and more and more isolated from the stream of vigorous life of which he was once a part.

His paper detailed census statistics and concluded that an ageing population was proved.

On local authority building rates at the time he gave a worrying estimate:

It is reliably estimated that the local authorities' present rate of building for the old will satisfy only one third of the need in the next twenty years. To illustrate, in Sheffield, living in Corporation dwellings there are 9,000 pensioners, and in addition there are over 8,000 old people on our list for a small flat, and this out of a population of just over half a million. These figures, however, tend to hide the real size of the problem because 4,700 of our pensioners live in family houses and at first sight it would seem logical to enormously increase the provision of one-bedroomed flats for these people, but that would merely store up trouble for the future when there would be large estates completely out of social balance, comprising as they would only old people.

As we know, the percentage of one-bedroomed dwellings for the aged has been increased since then, but the problem still remains and it is interesting to see that in 1964 Sheffield's waiting-list – 'over 8,000' – for old people's flats is roughly the same as at present.

The same arguments that are used today applied equally in 1964:

... It is obviously impossible to ignore the just demands of those families on our waiting-list and those others whom we are dispossessing from the slums. It is a difficult problem to tackle but with limited resources priorities have to be decided and only a proportion of one-bedroomed accommodation can be provided in any one year.

Mr Aldhous stressed the need for careful siting of old folk's housing

to give the old folk a sense of belonging to the community; their dwellings need to be near the centre of events on the estate, near the shops to minimize the physical effort of shopping, near the bus stop so they can easily travel to the town centre and visit their children. At the same time their blocks of flats should not be too large in number (so as to avoid a concentration of old people), nor be near children's playgrounds; four-bedroomed houses should be sited away from the old folk because such houses have large families and children at play can cause a great deal of annoyance to their grandparents.

Describing the type of building at that time the paper said:

Latterly we have built three-storey flats with the ground and first floors being used to house old people in one-bed flats and the top-floor flats have been given to single persons aged over forty. In our point blocks (thirteen storeys) half of their number has been granted to old people and out of twenty-two blocks of one-bed flats, comprising 1,056 dwellings, there are over four hundred living at all levels up to the thirteenth storey. In addition we have a hundred and seventy living in our Park Hill flats which, as you will know, rise to thirteen storeys too. I think this once and for all destroys the oft-expressed opinion that old folk will not live above ground. This demonstrates that they will. [Here Mr Aldhous added a most significant comment] ... *It would seem that the real objection is to climbing steps to gain access to their own dwellings, since obviously in the high blocks there are lifts.**

Mr Aldhous went on to give examples of the kind of safety fittings which can be installed into an old person's flat – 'Gas taps should be easily turned by an arthritic hand and there should be no confusion as to which tap controls which appliance ... pre-payment meters at ground level are a strain on an old back that is impossible in many cases to sustain' – and said, 'Practically every item in a house can be examined and made safe for the old to use.'

In ending his paper he related housing to welfare services:

These two, decent housing and domiciliary services, sustain the individual, prolonging his life, delaying the age when he asks for a place in a resident home where, as he gets older and more frail, he can expect a considerable amount of attention. Finally, of course, there comes the time when he can only be adequately cared for as a permanent bed patient in a geriatric ward of a hospital. It is significant that the provision of such beds is not to be increased; thus, our efforts must be turned to preserving a man's independence in his

Author's italics.

own home, greater emphasis being placed upon the three services as described, viz., adequate housing, efficient domiciliary services and residential homes. The problem is increasing and will continue to increase.

That paper contained a very real note of warning for the future and we are now seeing the result of failing to heed the warnings sounded by Mr Aldhous and others like him, not only in Sheffield, but throughout the country.

The warning was there regarding quantity – the present rate of building for the old would satisfy only one third of the need in the next twenty years. It was there with regard to safety and siting, and with regard to avoiding concentrations of old people. Since that paper was presented six years have gone by and as far as its waiting-list is concerned Sheffield is just as far from solving the problem of properly housing its aged. Although in those years Sheffield's stock of housing for old people has increased at a growing rate, included in the increase were many more flats with access staircases (Kelvin is such an example, as well as an example of great concentration), which in themselves have added to the problems.

Two of Mr Aldhous's points are arguable. Firstly, his reference to accommodation suitable for an active, newly-retired sixty-five-year-old presenting real problems fifteen or twenty years later. This is especially relevant when half of Sheffield's flats for old people have been built with access stairways. If dwellings are properly designed so that a semi-mobile eighty-year-old can live with as much comfort as his age and infirmity will allow, they will also be suitable for an active sixty-five-year-old. Therefore design should be right from the start.

Secondly, high flats. In 1964 living high in the air was still something of a novelty and in recent years has been subject to increasing criticism on sociological and environmental grounds, not only regarding elderly people but in relation to families as well. I would agree that some old people can live satisfactorily in high flats and for many the views from their windows are a constant source of enjoyment – especially in Sheffield where some of the tower blocks on the hillsides provide splendid panoramas of the city. But we now know that the thirteen-storey point blocks have contributed to the loneliness of old people and, for the old and the handicapped, the worst aspects of all of high living is when the lifts are out of order. The frequency with which they fail can cause great distress to old people. Some of them are afraid to go out for fear that on their return they will find the lift has broken down and they will be faced with a long struggle to climb endless flights of stairs.

An interesting, perhaps extreme, example concerned not an old-age pensioner but a fifty-three-year-old woman crippled with multiple sclerosis and confined to a wheelchair. She lived with her husband on the twelfth floor of a city-centre block and returned to find both lifts out of order. Unable to find the caretaker, the custodian of the telephone number of the lift engineers, her husband called the police and she was carried upstairs.

The woman complained that helpless people like herself should not be put in high flats when young couples lived on the ground floor. She had complained about the lifts before and had accepted a city-centre flat, rather than one on the outskirts, as the lesser of two evils. She said the hills on the outskirts would prevent her ever getting out.

Again the same conclusion has to be reached. There is not enough of the right type of accommodation in the right places and what has been provided has been built on the basis of insufficient information.

In the previous chapter I mentioned local authority dependence on Ministry subsidies and loan sanctions for building for the old (as for any other type of building). To qualify new developments have to keep within Parker Morris standards of quality and within the cost yardstick. From 1 November 1970 new, mandatory minimum standards applied to new schemes specifically designed for and intended for occupation by old people. Schemes only qualify for subsidy or loan sanction if they comply with the standards, but new, improved features now attract additional subsidy. These new mandatory minimum standards should substantially improve the quality of housing for old people. It is a pity that such standards were not laid down much earlier, for, as I have attempted to show, the need for such improvement, and therefore for increased subsidy, should have been recognized in this way a long time ago.

'The new mandatory minimum standards relate to all local authority housing for old people. In all cases there will be special provision for old people within the dwelling and these will take the form of a high standard of heating, certain safety measures and other aids,' said the Ministry of Housing and Local Government Circular which advised local authorities of the changes.

In the light of the old people's accommodation already built in Sheffield some of the new requirements make interesting reading. For example, in future all access stairs shall be enclosed; where access to a dwelling would involve a climb of more than one storey from the point of pedestrian and vehicular access (whichever is lower) a lift shall be provided; all access above four storeys shall be enclosed and two lifts shall be provided. In blocks of five or six storeys a minimum of twelve old people's dwellings on the fifth and sixth floors is considered necessary to justify a second lift. Old people, therefore, should not be accommodated on the fifth and sixth floors of such blocks unless this condition is met.

Other requirements relate to heating and minimum space standards and plans must show furniture drawn on. A list of the furniture which each room must be capable of holding is given. In the kitchen, standards regulate the height of shelves and working surfaces; in the bathroom it is demanded that all baths shall be flat-bottomed and of such length that an old person cannot become completely immersed (maximum length 5ft 1in) and that at least one hand-hold be provided, a condition also demanded of water-closets. Bathroom and WC doors must open outwards and be fitted with special locks which can be opened from outside. A similar series of standards are also laid down for grouped flatlets.

As well as outlining the increased subsidies to be given for these improvements in dwellings built to Parker Morris standards, the circular also outlines the rate of subsidy to be paid for optional extras, which, in old people's flats, may include the provision of a common-room with lavatory and kitchen, emergency alarm system and even a guest room.

Perhaps the most interesting section of all in this circular is a check-list offered as 'a guide to the special aspects of designing for old people's dwellings'.

An introduction to the check-list says:

It has to be remembered that most old people for whom housing is being provided will eventually be living alone and all housing for old people needs to be planned for sociability so as to avoid loneliness and isolation. This is particularly desirable where rehousing involves moving to a new area and, though the subject is outside the scope of this circular, good housing management practice can assist by keeping together groups of friends and neighbours as far as practicable.

The check-list asks questions such as:

Is the scheme conveniently sited in relation to

(a) Shops, bus stops, church, pub, post office? (Shopping may be the last activity and source of contact for old people; 0.6 km (¼ mile) should be maximum and the route should be safe from traffic and preferably avoiding steep gradients.)

(b) Ease of visiting by friends and relatives?

Are the dwellings sited away from disturbing noise?

Has the scheme been designed to make the best use of prospect, aspect and levels?

Do all dwellings get some sunshine for part of the day in living rooms and bedrooms?

Are there sheltered, sunny seats out of doors?

Have single steps, thresholds, winders and other hazards been avoided?

Not all the items in the check-list are mandatory requirements which must be met if a local authority is to qualify for subsidy or loan sanction. But some of the most significant are. Among them is: 'Are all access balconies well-sheltered and, in the case of dwellings above four storeys from ground, are they totally enclosed?'

Had such a requirement been in force at the time Park Hill, Hyde Park and more latterly Kelvin were planned, would they have been built to the present design? Or would it be argued that the decks, the 'streets in the sky', are not access balconies as such? Although this is something of a semantic argument I would say that, despite their depth and the protection they afford, the decks for this purpose should be classified as access balconies.

As I pointed out in the previous chapter, less than two months after extensive press criticism of the design of these blocks (on the thirteen steps in the old people's flats), plans for two projected deck-access developments were returned to the architects for redesigning to eliminate the stairs. These two projects involved a total of 207 dwellings. Unfortunately other plans for deck-access blocks involving hundreds of other dwellings were too far advanced to be sent back and all contain a proportion of dwellings for the old. But an assurance was given that further deck-access building would be planned to eliminate the interior staircases in the old folk's flats. If, in future, the decks are to be considered as balconies further redesigning may have to take place to enclose them above four storeys, or old people's dwellings must not be included above that height.

It is interesting too that the circular should comment on building for sociability to avoid loneliness and isolation. Again, where old people are concerned, not much can be said in favour of Park Hill, Hyde Park and Kelvin. To reach the deck an old person first has to climb the stairs, then the decks themselves present a long, often windswept aspect of rows of doors, which, including the turns as they follow the building, are as much as three hundred yards long. Over three hundred old people in one block, spread door by door along 'streets in the sky', is not my idea of the tight-knit, compact community which is desirable if the ideal of sociability in design is to be achieved. I would also suggest that this design puts a strain on a community which tries to help its elderly, whether voluntarily or statutorily. A block of over nine hundred flats of which one third are flats for the aged gives a heavy concentration of old folk.

Eliminating hazards is another question raised by the check-list. As it points out, a single step can be a hazard. So can a door-step when a wheelchair case is involved. In July 1969 a case was discovered of a sixty-six-year-old man, confined to a wheelchair, who was housebound because of a five-inch wooden doorstep to his ground-floor flat. He was unable to propel the chair over a ramp and his wife was unable to help because of arthritis in her hands. For two years he had repeatedly asked the Housing Department to remove the step. The answers he received bordered on the incredible. The Architect's Department said that if alterations needed to remove the step were only a small job there would be no hesitation in carrying them out. But the step was part of a frame holding the door and windows, and all this would have to come out. It was not simply a question of altering the height of the threshold. The Architect's Department thought the best course would be for the man and his seventy-year-old wife to move to another flat and therefore it was the job of housing management. Pressure brought personal inspection from a city councillor, the chief maintenance inspector of the Housing Department and an official of the Health Department. The result was that three days after the Architect's Department had, in effect, said it was too big a job, the Public Works Department removed the step, removed a course of bricks and some paving stones and replaced the step with one which could be raised on a hinge – all for a cost of 'less than £35'. Even then an official of the Architect's Department had the bad grace to comment : 'I can only think that even though his dwelling is now seemingly all right for him, they must have spoiled the terrace from a use point of view.'

Another inexcusable case was of an elderly cripple who was paralysed from the waist downwards. He had not been out of his terraced house for six years and did not have a wheelchair. One which had been provided was too high for him and he crawled around his house, sleeping in a chair because he could not get into bed. He too was one of the last to leave a slum clearance street and his case was widely publicized as an urgent need for rehousing and drawn to the attention of the Housing

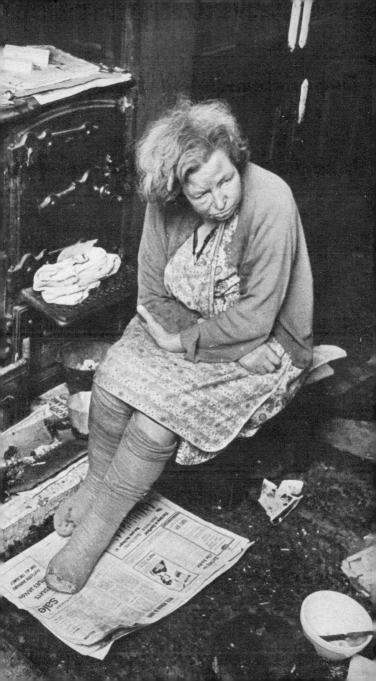

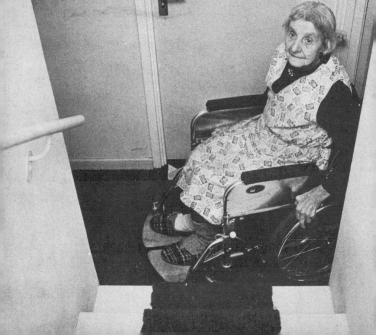

Department. He was speedily found a ground-floor flat, and in an area occupied by many of his former neighbours. He was also provided with a new and suitable wheelchair, only to find he could not propel it out of the flat because he needed ramps over his doorstep. He also found that he could not manoeuvre himself from the chair into his bed, something which he had been looking forward to for six years. He needed a form of hoist to do so.

Propelling a wheelchair over a small step may not sound like a big problem. It is in fact impossible. To prove the point one of *The Star*'s young reporters sat in the chair and tried to wheel it over the step. He could not do it. Similarly when he tried to push the chair and the old man over the obstacle he only succeeded with a struggle and there was a danger that the old man would fall out. Without a ramp the old man was a prisoner and, of course, it was soon provided.

This was an interesting case for other reasons. Despite his disability the old man was determined to be as independent as possible. In his previous home he had lived with the assistance of a home-help but had refused meals on wheels, preferring to crawl in to his kitchen and prepare food. He had also received visits from the home-nursing service. Apart from the fact that he should have been provided with a suitable wheelchair long before he was rehoused, why were his needs not properly examined at the time when he moved into his new flat? Why was it necessary to bring his case to the attention of the authorities again so that a ramp and a hoist could be provided for him?

Situations such as the two described – and there were others – are not good enough. Both show a lack of proper investigation and in the second case it can rightly be said that the case was inadequately investigated before, during and after the man's move to a new flat. And let us remember one other point: he was not being moved to a flat specially built for a physically handicapped person (there are too few of these to meet demand in any case). Is it not reasonable and necessary therefore to look at the condition of the person and see how the flat can be adapted to meet his needs?

The big city, with its vast new urban communities, its massive slum-clearance programme and a bigger bureaucratic machine, appears to be more likely to throw up problems of this kind. With its rehousing programme dictated to a large extent by financial compromise, compromises must also be made with the design of buildings for old people. This has quite clearly happened in the past and seems likely to happen in the future.

The financial demands on a large urban authority are many. Public transport is now in a state of flux and it is even being suggested that it be fully subsidized from rates; wage bills are soaring for all classes of local authority employee; control of air and river pollution becomes more important; people are demanding better and better environments and not only the cost of labour but material costs also rise continually. In the financial year 1970–71 Sheffield's budget estimated an extra £3,700,000 just to stand still, to pay for rising costs while present services were not improved or expanded.

Some local authorities, however, often rural or small urban districts, have less widespread demands on their financial resources, fewer social pressures within the community and better and more available land on which to build. They often have a better record in housing the old and thus we get a disparity in both quantity and quality of services for the elderly in adjacent areas.

Many of the smaller authorities around Sheffield have been able to take a much more comprehensive view of providing special fittings for old people in occupation of their flats and bungalows. Some, with the topographical advantage of flatter building land, had all their old people accommodated at ground level. But perhaps the best comparisons can be made with the larger urban authorities.

Barnsley, hilly and industrial, with a population of 74,880 and an elderly population estimated at 9,200, had 1,400 purpose-built dwellings for the old in occupation, 110 in the course of erection and 479 other dwellings convenient for the old. Its waiting-list was about seven hundred. More than eighty per cent of its accommodation for the old contained special baths or low baths with handrails, the majority had power points which could be operated without stooping, and handrails were provided on ramped paths. None of this accommodation had access staircases.

Sheffield's nearest neighbour Rotherham Borough estimated that seventeen per cent of its population of 86,450 were pensioners. It provided six hundred bungalows and over 1,200 flats, maisonettes and bedsitters suitable for old people. Some of the flats and bungalows had been built specially to offer a large number of features to aid infirm people such as oversized rooms and doors for wheelchair traffic, split-level cooking arrangements, cantilevered worktops in kitchens, large handles on doors, cantilevered lavatories, low baths, grip handles, shower sprays and cord-operated windows. Accommodation with access stairs was only allocated to aged people who said they were able to climb them, but the demand for ground-floor accommodation was far in excess of supply.

Rotherham Borough had 1,200 old people living in three-bedroomed houses and over the next five years the number of smaller dwellings would be increased to release some of these under-occupied houses for families.

Both these towns, although considerably smaller in population, have similar problems of slum clearance and urban renewal to Sheffield, but their performance in housing old people has obviously been better.

In looking at over twenty local authorities around Sheffield we found that no serious attempt was made to defend designs which had access staircases although quite a number of the local authorities had been forced to build with them. Rawmarsh Urban District, for example, with a population of 19,600, said it had few cases where old people had to use access staircases but kept a special list of those who had.

The survey of smaller authorities proved that usually they had been able to provide better housing in quantity and quality than the big city and this difference was even more marked in the provision of warden services for the old, which, together with sheltered flatlet schemes, will be discussed later.

With an increasingly elderly population of which a growing number will be in the over-seventy-five age group, one can only conclude that in years to come the City of Sheffield is going to regret building so many dwellings for the elderly with exterior or interior access stairways. So are other authorities which have built similar flats. But in Sheffield the policy continues at least as long as new housing schemes coming into the pipeline are of similar design to those already erected. It takes a long time to bring forward new designs, but if the care of the elderly in Sheffield is to be improved from a housing point of view, many more homes with a level entrance must be provided. While the new mandatory minimum standards which took effect in November 1970 must improve the standard of interior fittings and safety aids for old people, in my view they did not go far enough. They should have demanded access from a level entrance or that level entrances should be provided for the vast majority of old people's dwellings.

Eight

'We Never Feel Lonely'

Many old people, while unable to lead fully independent lives in their own homes, are not necessarily candidates for a place in a residential home. An old folk's home, although it is now a modern cheerful place and should no longer carry the stigma of an institution, withdraws the aged from the wider society they might encounter outside. Therefore between fully independent living and the residential home there is a place for a type of housing which provides for those old people who are still capable of living within a community but at the same time need, and indeed welcome, a degree of supervision.

What are generally termed 'sheltered' housing schemes have provided the answer. But at the moment it is only a limited answer because sheltered flatlet and bungalow schemes are few in comparison to the numbers who need them.

In its annual report for 1969 Help the Aged said that of the 1,500,000 old people who live alone in this country '300,000 are in urgent need of sheltered housing, that is, flatlets with a warden on hand in case of need'. Most of the work of Help the Aged in this country is directed to providing such sheltered housing and it is now the largest specialist housing charity of its type in Britain. By the end of 1969 it had £3,000,000-worth of housing in hand for the elderly, although its officials freely admit that this is only scratching the surface of the problem. Nevertheless, housing the old is a matter in which every little helps and the completed schemes of Help the Aged provide some of the finest examples in the country of sheltered housing for old people.

Sheltered housing creates a pleasant community environment

for old people in which they support each other and are supported by the services of a resident warden. Between thirty and forty flatlets are considered the ideal for such a scheme, which can include larger flatlets for elderly couples, rather than just homes for single old people. The flatlets should be grouped around communal facilities, e.g. a comfortable common-room with television, lavatory and kitchen, a laundry with automatic washing machines and dryers, a garden with wind-protected outdoor seating. Ideally, each flatlet should have its own bath as well as WC and although Help the Aged now puts a bathroom in all its flatlets, common bathrooms are allowed by Ministry of Housing and Local Government standards for local authority schemes.

The advantages are many, and some authorities, not least Help the Aged, suggest that sheltered flatlet schemes could take the place of residential homes in future planning for old people. For example, when an old person is taken into the care of a residential home, he or she must sell up his former home and give up possessions which have the value of sentiment and familiarity. In a flatlet scheme they can retain them. Nor are they dependent on meals provided by the home. They can cook what they want as they want, or the meals-on-wheels service can provide for them in the normal way. However, while I believe that some of the people presently taken into fully residential care could be accommodated properly in a sheltered flatlet scheme, I do not believe they can fully replace the intensive support which a residential home can give.

Flatlet schemes may also include a guest room for visitors who have to travel long distances, or where a younger relative may stay while caring for one of the old people who is sick. Government subsidy can now be paid for providing a guest room in local-authority sheltered-flatlet schemes.

From an economic point of view they also have advantages. According to Help the Aged it costs about £15 a week to keep one old person in a residential home. They reckon that the support a local welfare authority needs give to one of their schemes costs about £2,000 a year. They claim that in economic terms alone sheltered housing is one of the biggest bargains welfare authorities have ever looked at.

In rural areas, sheltered housing can be provided by having bungalows grouped around communal facilities, but in urban areas flatlets are likely to be a more feasible proposition. Again, there is a distinct advantage which Help the Aged has proved by example. A scheme of thirty-plus flatlets with a three-bedroomed flat for the warden and his family need occupy only half an acre of ground. Help the Aged designs each scheme to suit the land available and say they can make use of small sites which have been virtually forgotten by the local authority, whose planning department is usually concerned with much bigger comprehensive developments.

A typical example of this was when Help the Aged asked one local authority for sites and were offered a number, all over one acre in size. At the request of the charity a brief check by a junior in the surveyor's office quickly produced three other smaller sites, which had been overlooked. In fact, Help the Aged complains that many local authorities, especially the big ones, are slow, even reluctant, to offer sites. For its part the charity tries to demonstrate how, through tailoring its designs to fit the land, sites which are regarded as difficult or even useless can be made to accommodate a flatlet scheme for the old.

Help the Aged approached Sheffield City Council in February 1970 and, although in March the City Council resolved to 'give the utmost assistance' to voluntary housing associations to help house old people, the charity was still waiting at the end of the year for Sheffield to suggest possible building sites. Sites have now been allocated.

This charity firmly believes that the difficult sites on which they are prepared to build are to be found in abundance in large urban areas. But in the large urban areas, where the need is greatest, the local authorities seem to be the most reluctant to offer sites. In effect, the complaint is of bureaucratic inertia.

An example of Help the Aged's work is at Aldershot where a scheme of thirty flatlets – two storeys – was built on the site of a derelict graveyard for £75,000. Aldershot Borough Council provided the site for a peppercorn rent and arranged a sixty-year mortgage. The interest rate on this is kept down to four per cent by an annual Government grant which is available for such projects. The welfare authority, in this case Hampshire County Council, make a grant of £5 a year for every flat. The rest of the running costs, including the warden's wages, are paid for partly from the charity's national funds and partly by direct local appeals. A committee of five local people, including a building society accountant and a bank manager, handles local finances.

Local authorities are now in a better position to build improved flatlet schemes as a result of increased subsidies and better standards set out in the Ministry of Housing and Local Government circular described in the previous chapter. Some have provided schemes of this sort in the past and others, like Sheffield, are now moving towards quantity provision of this service to the old.

In considering how successful this kind of accommodation can be, we can look at a development in Sheffield at a district called Lowedges where thirty-one self-contained flatlets are built around communal facilities and a pleasant rose garden.

Twenty-three single old people and seven married couples live in the flats, which open on to warm, covered halls. All the flatlets have a fitted kitchen with a water closet and handbasin, while bathrooms are shared by three or four tenants. The communal sitting-room is approached by covered passageways. The old people who live there are happy and content, the crushing problem of loneliness defeated. Any one of the elderly tenants who 'wants a bit of company' has only to sit in the communal lounge and others will be there before much time has passed. 'We never feel lonely,' said a 70-year-old woman. 'We have our own homes to go to if we want to be private, but there's always someone nearby if we want to talk.' One old man of seventy-five has become the organizer of bingo evenings and fish-and-chip suppers and in summer arranges coach outings to the Derbyshire countryside. Home helps visit as they would any old person anywhere in Sheffield and district nurses attend those with disabilities. Such schemes have all the appearance of providing a near-ideal solution for housing old people, especially the lonely among them. This grouped flatlet scheme is much appreciated by its residents even though it was built before local authorities were required to provide an alarm system connecting each flat with caretaker's or warden's quarters. There is a resident caretaker.

At the beginning of 1970 this was the only sheltered flatlet scheme in occupation in Sheffield. One other scheme was nearing completion and two others were to be started. Six more schemes above the normal building programme were to go ahead and, later in the year, seven more were being investigated.

In the present provision of sheltered, supervised flatlet and bungalow schemes, we again see a disparity between the big city and the smaller urban and rural authorities. Illustrating this disparity is not intended as a criticism of the big city, but to show how widely services for the elderly can vary, and give weight to arguments that the big urban areas have special problems to overcome.

Initially it was discovered that all the local authorities around Sheffield provided more wardens for the old per head. Some were resident wardens, whose duties were with grouped bungalow and flatlet schemes, others were travelling wardens. Chesterfield Rural District (population approximately 74,000) had three 'precinct' schemes with three wardens and a total of fifty-seven dwellings ; Rotherham Borough had six grouped schemes totalling 185 dwellings, where old people had the benefit of communal, television-fitted lounges and inter-com systems from their own homes to wardens' quarters. Three more such schemes were in the pipeline. Rotherham Rural District, with a population of 68,000, employed sixty-two wardens and had seven schemes of grouped bungalows with resident wardens. Dodworth Urban District, with a population of only 4,340, had six community centres with resident wardens to help old people and ten travelling wardens. Both these last two areas said that every old person whom they knew lived alone was visited every day seven days a week by wardens if they wished. Barnsley, with a population of 74,000, employed thirty-eight wardens and Hoyland Urban District, population 16,000, employed twenty-seven.

A rough table gives an example of the employment of wardens in some areas around Sheffield.

Dodworth U D C	one warden to 300 of population
Hoyland U D C	one to 600
Darton U D C	one to 1,000
Rotherham R D C	one to just over 1,000
Stocksbridge U D C	one to 1,450
Barnsley	one to 2,000
Cudworth U D C	one to 2,300
Wortley R D C	one to 2,350
Staveley U D C	one to 2,500
Maltby U D C	one to 2,500

At the beginning of 1970 Sheffield employed forty-three wardens, roughly one to 11,500 per head of population. Budget estimates provided for employing twenty-four more wardens to a total of sixty-seven, but at the end of the year this still left Sheffield with an average of only one to 8,000 of population.

The provision of wardens is in itself inseparable from the provision of sheltered housing schemes for the old. Obviously, the task of wardening old people is made easier by properly designed sheltered housing and all the local authorities around Sheffield needed more sheltered bungalows and flatlets, Rotherham Borough estimating that it required another four hundred places in wardened community schemes.

Regular visits by wardens to old people who live in their own flats and houses can add a great deal to their feeling of security, giving them an important sense of not being alone in the world. As the value of this service has become more widely understood Sheffield's Health and Welfare Department has faced regular appeals for wardens in areas where there are none, although sometimes these appeals have been made because the old folk have been put in a state of fear and insecurity by the activities of young vandals. A demand was also regularly made for alarm systems connecting old folk's flats to wardens' quarters of which, at the beginning of 1970, Sheffield Corporation had none.

Rotherham Rural District provides an example of a first-class warden system for old people who live alone. It is based on the seventeen parishes of the district and the wardens, usually middle-aged married women, visit the old people in their own parishes. Because of their close contacts in the parish communities in which they worked the wardens were able to arrange visiting schedules according to local circumstances. Furthermore, having been built up over four and a half years, a backup service of sixty-two relief wardens had been established to ensure that visiting continued even when the full-time warden was ill or on holiday. This type of community involvement led to much more than an official round of duty ; genuine, affectionate care had resulted. For this the wardens received £4 10s. a week, of which almost the total cost was covered by West Riding County Council grant.

Rotherham Rural District felt it had something to boast about with a service which provided daily visits seven days a week for every old person living alone. But such a visiting service would be almost impossible to emulate in a big city where housing itself and a much-needed expansion of the services provided by professional, trained social workers and health visitors must, for financial reasons, take their place in the order of priorities ahead of the employment of wardens. But it clearly appears that warden services are easier to provide and more efficient in operation in the parish communities of a rural district where everyone knows his neighbours well. As a job it is less attractive and more difficult in the large urban area with its sprawling estates of new houses or concentrations of tower blocks, where a deep sense of community will take a long time to develop and will perhaps never develop to the same extent as in a rural village.

Again, this is evidence that the big city has greater and more complex problems to solve in providing good housing and the necessary ancillary services for old people than the smaller, closer community. It is far too easy to say Sheffield ought to be able to provide just as good a warden service as Rotherham Rural District. To do so would be to ignore the much wider social problems of the big city, which is bound to seek a steady expansion of social services on a broad and often costly front. In concentrating on an expansion in, say, warden services, Sheffield would probably have to move more slowly on another aspect of caring for the elderly.

With this kind of situation in mind, there are sound reasons why many smaller authorities do not wish to be swallowed by the big authorities under proposals for reorganizing local government. Not only would they lose autonomy, but their smaller, local problems would lose priority to the more urgent needs of the big cities.

Not all groupings of bungalows and flatlets can properly be described as 'sheltered' housing as the term is now understood and where a warden and communal facilities are a requirement. But they are a great improvement on what has gone before. Sheffield's scheme at Lowedges, even though its caretaker had instructions not to take responsibility for the old people and even though it does not have an alarm system, proved the value of creating such a community for its aged tenants.

But such communities need cooperation between housing and welfare departments to make them a success. The Seebohm report is of the opinion that sheltered housing should primarily remain the responsibility of housing departments but feels it should be extended, where necessary, to cover households containing mentally or physically handicapped members as well as old people. Such an extension would increase the need for welfare and housing cooperation, but even for the elderly a balanced community must be created between those who are reasonably sprightly and those handicapped by age and increasing infirmity.

Because the debilitating effects of loneliness are removed by sheltered housing and because they can become self-sustaining communities, the strain on the rest of the population and on the social services must be decreased by its provision. In fact, sheltered housing can be seen as epitomizing what the Seebohm Report meant when it said good accommodation was the key to the successful provision of other kinds of services for old people.

The local authority is, and must be, the major provider of this and other kinds of housing for the old. This is especially true in the big industrial cities. Those who have financial independence in old age seek to retire to cottages and bungalows in the fresh air of the country or the seaside; others can pay for their own care in privately-run old folk's homes. But the many thousands who cannot afford this look to the local authority to provide. No body but a local authority could today attempt the large-scale building of dwellings for the old, but I have drawn attention to the activities of Help the Aged to show that such housing charities can, and do, add to the diversity of accommodation available for the elderly.

However, they need to be encouraged by the local authority and it is quite true to say that Help the Aged has had a number of frustrating experiences in its dealings with town halls. The Seebohm Report agrees. 'Far too little attention has been paid to the encouragement of housing associations,' it says, and goes on, 'There is real value in providing some alternative choice for old people between types of housing management and since, on the whole, very few houses to let are built by private enterprise, the housing association must be the major alternative to the local authority.'

The specialist provision of Help the Aged provides an example of the alternative. At the end of 1969 it had completed ten sheltered-flatlet schemes, six under construction, eighteen to be started in 1970 and fourteen at an advanced stage of negotiation. Obviously this is a very valuable contribution, even though it is only small in comparison to the overall need for both flats and sheltered housing. It is particularly valuable because of its imaginative use of otherwise valueless plots of land

and because it is a demonstration of the kind of properly designed, purpose-built housing for old people which local authorities ought to provide in quantity in years to come.

It is now quite clear that many old people prefer to live in this kind of accommodation or with the support of a warden. The provision of warden services is developing quite rapidly and must continue to increase. It is estimated that by 1971 159,000 units of accommodation will have the support of wardens compared with a 1965 total of 63,000. And despite the present financial and recruiting limitations on the extent of warden provision, cities like Sheffield must seek to give the security of warden services to a much greater number of old people.

Nine

A Desperate Shortage

At the heart of Sheffield's problem of caring for its old folk is its desperate shortage of places in residential homes. It was this shortage which caused Dr Lambie to refer to Sheffield as a 'geriatric slum', and, compared to the elderly population, the number of places in old folk's homes in Sheffield is the lowest of any major city in the country.

Many present-day old folk's homes are in no way comparable to the grim institutions of Poor Law times. They can be pleasant, modern and comfortable places which usually provide between thirty and fifty places, compared to the large numbers (150 and more in some cases) who used to be virtually prisoners in the old workhouses. Certainly, there need be now no reason to think of old people as being shut away and, indeed, public attitudes have changed a great deal since 1948 when welfare authorities were given the duty of providing such homes under Part III of the National Assistance Act. Since then local authorities have aimed to replace the old institutions with new, purpose-built homes for the old, a process which should be completed within a few years. There are exceptions but, despite the replacements and the general increase in the building of old people's homes throughout the country, at present little over two per cent of the nation's elderly population is accommodated in old people's homes. In Sheffield the figure is around one per cent.

The old folk's home is fully sheltered housing for the elderly and an admission that their independence can no longer be preserved either by the help of family, friends and local-authority welfare services. Its importance lies mainly in its relationship with hospital geriatric services and a shortage of places in old folk's homes can have a significant bearing on hospital geriatric care.

We have already seen that family doctors in Sheffield are bitterly critical of the local authority for its failure to provide more residential homes for the aged, and indeed their condemnation would seem to be unanimous. They are agreed that many old people need greater shelter than can be provided in their own, often inadequate, homes and yet waiting-lists are such that only the most desperate need will produce a place in a residential home.

At the beginning of 1970 Sheffield had twenty residential homes provided by the Social Care Department with a total of 740 places plus thirty-seven short-stay beds. Three more were to be completed in 1970, adding 138 places. The emergency application which led the Department of Health and Social Security to agree to Sheffield building a total of ten new homes in three years, instead of the six it would normally contemplate, would add a total of four hundred beds over three years. But at the time the waiting-list for admission had grown to 1,079, of which 363 were classified as being in immediate need.

This increase, in places, it was claimed, would bring Sheffield up to the national average, a statement which was repeated for me by a spokesman for the Department in September 1970, but which cannot be true. The discrepancy, which was pointed out by a consultant physician in geriatric medicine at a Sheffield hospital, is quite simply calculated on the number of available beds and the elderly population of Sheffield.

Assuming Sheffield has an elderly population of 70,000 (1966 Sample Census) the very best estimate for Sheffield at the end of three years is roughly seventeen places per thousand of elderly population, although the Department claimed Sheffield would have achieved a national average of 'about twenty'. This calculation, of course, takes no account of the predicted absolute rise in the elderly population or the big increase in over-seventy-fives. According to the Department Sheffield had 'about fourteen' beds per thousand elderly in 1970, compared to a national average of 'about eighteen'.

The Department refused to confirm or deny comparative figures for the other towns and cities, saying such comparisons were for 'internal use'. These figures produced by the consultant geriatrician showed that by 1971 Newcastle would have 23·3 beds per thousand elderly, Leeds 24·4, Birmingham 18·2, Liverpool 20·7 and Manchester 27·2.

These figures show how far Sheffield has to go to catch up with other industrial cities and, indeed, expert medical opinion in Sheffield takes the view that the city needs to double its provision of old folk's homes. All the doctors I spoke to laid emphasis on the relationship between hospital geriatric care and old folk's homes. Guidance to hospitals and local authorities was given by a Ministry of Health circular in 1965, which said local authorities were expected to provide the health services a person could expect if he were living in good circumstances in his own home, while hospitals were expected to care for the acutely ill, to provide short-term treatment, and were generally for those needing continuous medical treatment or nursing care which could not properly be given in their own homes. This circular asked hospitals and local authorities to make joint plans to admit people to the proper place from the outset and assess the scale of local provisions which each should provide.

Sheffield has two geriatric units at the Nether Edge and Northern General Hospitals, which between them have seven hundred beds for old people and a waiting-list which usually hovers around the two hundred mark. It is planned to increase the number of beds by two hundred over the next ten years, but whether this will be enough to cater for rising demand remains to be seen. The hospital doctors complain that because of the shortage of places in residential homes the hospital care of the elderly is blocked. As one put it: 'Doctors and nurses waste much of their time caring for patients whose only real needs are a bed and three square meals a day.' They are looking after old people in hospital because there is nowhere else for them to go.

The hospitals make the point that old people ought only to be admitted if they need the treatment that only a hospital can give. It was not the job of hospitals to provide sheltered care for old people. One house doctor suggested that on occasions general practitioners would exaggerate an old person's complaints to get him out of bad home conditions and into hospital. While the hospital doctors sympathized with the family doctors, they felt that hospital beds had to be reserved for those in need of medical treatment, particularly when there was a continual waiting-list for such treatment.

This situation is not peculiar to Sheffield. It happens in many areas. Barnsley's annual health report for 1969 pointed out that elderly people with problems which were sometimes predominantly social had to be admitted to hospital. As a result elderly people needing medical treatment were sometimes kept waiting so long that they deteriorated beyond recovery. Then they became permanent occupants of hospital beds.

This report also condemned the practice of admitting elderly patients known to be suffering from incurable diseases into hospital to die. 'This practice not only blocks valuable hospital beds but a point of more serious concern is the effect of such dying patients on the morale of other patients in the process of recovery,' said the report.

After hospital treatment the discharge of elderly patients is sometimes impossible to arrange. Although there is no medical reason for them to remain in hospital there is nowhere for them to go where they can be cared for. A geriatrician in Sheffield told me he had many patients who would benefit from being discharged from hospital and placed in a residential home. The hospital atmosphere, with the sick and dying all around, was not the place for old people once they were fit enough to leave. But they stayed because there were no places for them in local-authority residential homes.

A number of cases were recorded where old people had to wait for the hospital beds they obviously needed promptly. In one a ninety-four-year-old woman, senile and living alone, had fallen and injured herself on a number of occasions. She was once found lying on the floor beside an armchair which had caught fire. Her doctor had repeatedly tried to get her into hospital, but without success. In this case she may well not have needed medical treatment and could have been cared for in an old folk's home. In another case a family doctor had found it impossible to arrange hospital admission for an old woman living alone who was almost blind and subject to blackouts and falls. Other cases showed the plight of old people newly released from hospital but not properly able to care for themselves in their own homes. Nor are the domiciliary services of health and welfare departments properly equipped to provide the kind of convalescent care such old people need.

It is a widely held misconception that the work of hospital geriatric units is to care for those who cannot look after themselves. Their function is, in fact, purely medical, to care for those who need continuous nursing which could not be given in their own homes, or to provide treatment, operations, therapy, etc., and to make old people fit for a return to life in the community. But even after the hospital has discharged its function some convalescent old people need greater shelter than can be provided in their own homes. Despite the efforts of local-authority domiciliary services, release to their lonely homes is often unsatisfactory and can sometimes lead to hospital readmission.

The Seebohm Report said:

We regard as extremely important the link between residential homes and hospitals. The common practice of a one for one exchange between homes and hospital, which seems to be the only way of getting from one to the other in so many places, may be largely due to an overall shortage of beds in the area. It is, however, quite unacceptable if hospitals and homes are to be used for their true purpose and, at the same time, it tends to place a resident in a home in a more favourable position to obtain a hospital bed than an old person in equal need living in his own home. In this area involving both medical and social care we consider that far more use than now should be made of the advice and services of the medical officer of health and the geriatric physician. Both have a contribution to make in the selection of residents to homes in the first place. We must rely on both, and particularly on the geriatric physician in the present situation, working with the head of the social service department to achieve what coordination they can in the residential and institutional fields by informal methods but we believe that, for the long term, nothing short of a reconstruction of the National Health Service and its relationships with local authority services will serve.

One of the stated objectives of Mr Richard Crossman's 1970 Green Paper, *The Future Structure of the National Health Service*, which obviously owes much of its inspiration to Seebohm, was to establish close links between the National Health Service and the public health and social services provided by local government.

Making out a case for unifying the health service, it referred to practical consequences resulting from a multiplicity of authorities.

First they impede the ultimate aim of meeting the needs of individual patients and their families comprehensively. Secondly, the limited resources provided for the National Health Service are at risk of being wasted or used to less than full advantage. For example, at heavy cost the hospital cares for patients who could well be treated at home if the right local services were available on a large enough scale. Many patients are in hospital who could live outside, would prefer to live outside and would fare better outside. In many such cases care at home with the support of the community health services would be the better and cheaper solution. At the same time other patients who really need care in hospital make demands on the local authority services while they wait to be admitted.

In its proposed reconstruction of the National Health Service, the Green Paper followed Seebohm's suggestion of the establishment of 'community physicians'.

Out of such a change might arise a community physician with a far wider and more responsible role than we have suggested above for a geriatric physician and the medical officer of health as a temporary measure. Through the community physician there would be links with general practitioners, dental and ophthalmic services, home nurses, medical social workers and health visitors and, particularly, with mental health services and hospital geriatric units. Old people may need any or all of these services at different times. Again, his help might be needed in the follow-up of discharged hospital patients to see that their needs were known and understood by the local authority home care services. In all, there is a need for imaginative ideas, for trying new approaches and a refusal to be satisfied with any particular method, merely because it has always been used in the past.

The Seebohm Report made a case for unifying local authority social services under a director of social services, which will come about in April 1971 as a result of the Local Authority Social Services Act 1970, and a case for reconstructing the National Health Service is made out in the Green Paper. Summarized, this saw the establishment of area health authorities, which would end the present tripartite service, that is, hospitals, family doctoring and local-authority services. Instead, area health authorities would administer every service to do with health, including general practice and some of those at present administered by local authorities such as the surveillance of community health and including those directly affecting old people – health centres, health visiting, home nursing and residential accommodation for those needing continuing medical supervision and not ready to live in the community.

Plans such as these ought to lead to a much-needed improvement in the coordination of services. But obviously, with the extremely unsatisfactory provision of places in old folk's homes in Sheffield, proper cooperation and coordination as suggested by Seebohm, or, indeed, the joint plans between hospital and local authority to admit people to the proper place from the outset as requested by the 1965 Ministry of Health circular, are very largely impossible. Certainly, the present relationship between geriatric units, old folk's homes and family doctors in Sheffield needs improving and can only be improved if their cooperation and coordination is helped by a greater number of available places in old people's residential homes and when the pressure on their services is relieved in this way.

How badly are more geriatric beds needed in hospitals? Sheffield has about average – one bed per thousand of elderly population – but from the family doctors' point of view and with the difficulty of arranging admissions and the length of time some old people have to wait, more are needed. Perhaps they would welcome any provision which would help them get frail and unwell old people into places where they can be properly cared for. Unfortunately more geriatric beds cannot be provided immediately. 'If we were given wards with two hundred more beds tomorrow they'd be no use to us,' said a geriatrician. 'We couldn't staff them.' For this reason, if for no other, increased provision of geriatric beds will have to be a gradual process.

The importance of the old folk's home in its relationship to hospital treatment was further illustrated by an article which appeared in the January 1970 issue of the *Lancet* in which Dr N. H. Nisbet, a consultant geriatrician at a Glasgow hospital, described the results of a survey which indicated that discharge home, either to live alone or with relatives, was often unsatisfactory.

Dr Nisbet questioned the fundamental aim of geriatric units of restoring old people to physical independence only to discharge them home: 'I am becoming increasingly worried whether this policy really benefits either the elderly patients or his relatives, and whether we are not putting an intolerable strain on the community.'

Dr Nisbet's investigations revealed that many relatives had been under severe strain from caring for old people and talked emotively of the 'ever-widening circles of strain caused by the illness of one old person. More and more people are sucked into this whirlpool of misery.'

Of fifty patients discharged home only fifteen were really happy to be leaving hospital ; twelve were returned to live alone and sixteen were reluctant to leave at all. In only nine cases could it be said the relatives were genuinely pleased to have them back.

Dr Nisbet concluded: 'It is no solution at all to insist on scattering such patients to individual private households where their apathy and helplessness will drag down the whole household.'

This report suggested that a great variety of accommodation

for the unfit elderly was needed and urged the provision of more sheltered housing, day hospitals, local-authority homes and longer-term hospital beds. More effort should also be made to help the elderly live independently instead of urging over-burdened relatives to take care of them.

Seebohm speaks of the need for 'imaginative ideas' and 'new approaches', and it would be interesting to see what impact the much wider provision of sheltered-flatlet schemes with a war-den in residence, as discussed in the previous chapter, would have on the present unsatisfactory relationship between geriat-ric unit and local-authority residential homes. Help the Aged holds the view that, if properly wardened, they can support old people newly released from hospital and it is easy to see how they can provide a much more satisfactory environment than if an old person were released to his own lonely home, perhaps to rely on no more than a daily visit from a home help and a weekly visit from the district nurse. On the other hand, could sheltered housing successfully take many of the old people who are now given and now seek places in residential homes and thus leave the homes with more capacity to undertake intensive support? If this were to prove feasible, sheltered-flatlet schemes, less expensive to run than old folk's homes, might ease the pressure on residential homes and allow the closer cooperation and coordination with hospital geriatric units which ought to be achieved. This is the kind of solution local authorities may well have to seek because of the difficulties of staffing residential homes which was demonstrated by the Williams Committee Report of 1967.

There is another category of old people for whom special residential care is needed – the mentally infirm aged. In Shef-field such statutory provision is non-existent. A Sheffield geria-trician estimated that the city needed three residential homes for psycho-geriatric cases, patients he described as 'the active wan-dering dement', the elderly person who has become senile and forgetful but who can still get out and about. As with the hous-ing needs of old people, so for the mentally infirm aged: we have far too little information.

The Seebohm Report said:

... We are especially concerned with the widespread failure to meet the current or future needs in the care of the mentally infirm aged. A far closer link must be forged between doctor and social worker, between hospital and local authority, indeed between all those who have any concern for the care of old people and their families. There are some old people in this category who need treatment; there are others who require only supervision, patience and understanding. Suitable accommodation is essential but, at present, seldom available. In theory responsibility is now shared between hospital and local authority; in practice it is not always accepted by either. It is in this field that the social service department has one of its major tasks before it. The Mental Health Act 1959 shifted the whole emphasis of care for the mentally infirm, including the aged, from institutional care to community care. There is still, however, in most places, a grave shortage of suitable accommodation for the mentally infirm aged, while community care is little more than a phrase in many areas.

In a later paragraph Seebohm comments:

It is clear that there is no hope in the foreseeable future of offering conventional psychiatric or social person to person service to all adults and children who are seriously maladjusted. Several studies have shown that there are far more old people with serious mental disorder living in their own homes than in all institutions together. We are only beginning to appreciate the dimensions of the 'psycho-geriatric' problem, but its difficulties are already plain.

Seebohm adds a footnote on the rising number of old people in mental institutions, pointing out that in 1954 there were 15,557 residents aged over seventy-five in mental hospitals who had been there for more than six months. By 1963 there were 21,171. 'How many of these people could be living in the community is another question; some of them could,' it says.

Local authorities have powers to provide residential accommodation for the mentally disordered, including the aged, under both health and welfare functions. For the aged such accommodation is generally provided under a local authority's welfare powers, but little such accommodation is available. Seebohm pointed out that over 13,000 mentally infirm people, mostly elderly, were living in such homes, and more specialized accommodation of this type will be needed in future if the size of the psycho-geriatric problem is as great as has been suggested.

Our own investigators estimated that among the many old people we saw in Sheffield during 1970 mental infirmity was present in about one in five. This was a layman's estimation, a commonsense view reached as a result of encountering irrational behaviour and people's inability to comprehend the world about them, and is in no way intended to suggest that all old people who display a degree of irrationality should be in residential care. It would seem fair to suggest that the number who should be in residential care as a result of mental infirmity is quite small and that the criteria for an old person's being taken into care should be inability to look after himself.

A number of examples of the 'active wandering dement' were recorded. These are not only a source of worry because they cannot take care of themselves, but are often a nuisance to neighbours who are, more than likely, old people themselves. One such case was tragic. The seventy-eight-year-old widow concerned lived on a crescent of pre-war old people's flats and was well known to the local-authority social services. She was receiving twice-weekly assistance from a home help, but had been abusive and refused to let the home help into her flat. Elderly neighbours said she was likely to be found wandering at all hours of the day or night, sometimes knocking at their doors and begging for food. One old neighbour took her food three times a week and all the neighbours we questioned were of the opinion she should have been in a hospital or hostel. One cold morning she was found dead of a heart attack in the driveway of a house about two hundred yards from her flat. This case exemplified the need for residential homes for the mentally disordered aged and the need to provide properly sheltered care for such old people. It is worth noting too that the group of flats where she lived had been without a warden for over a year since the retirement of the previous warden.

But what is mental infirmity in old people? Do we ascribe

the term mentally disordered to those we have previously called cantankerous, difficult or eccentric? Is it a sign of mental disorder when an old person refuses to open his door to social workers and determinedly continues to live in dirty, inadequate conditions?

Old people who leave pans to boil dry on their cookers and who are quite clearly a danger to themselves with fires, gas and electrical appliances may be senile or mentally infirm. But is this the 'serious mental disorder' to which Seebohm refers? It seems to me that it is not: but it is an argument for improved provision of sheltered care, whether residential or wardened flatlet schemes.

On the other hand, the cantankerous, difficult or eccentric old person may well be suffering from serious mental disorder, as may the old person who, to all intents and purposes, has withdrawn from the world. Writing purely as a layman it would be presumptuous for me to suggest that at the root of many psycho-geriatric problems is loneliness, lack of companionship or an old person's belief, right or wrong, that his children no longer care for him and cannot be bothered to visit.

As the 1959 Mental Health Act shifted the emphasis to communal rather than institutional care, the pattern of what society must try to achieve for the mentally disordered elderly fits what we are trying to do for old people in the normal course of events. If they are capable of living within the community they should be allowed to do so. Those who are not mentally capable of independent living, however, should be treated in residential care and not, as sometimes happens, occupy a medical bed in a hospital geriatric unit.

In dealing with all problems relating to the care of the elderly the aim of statutory and voluntary services has long been defined as the preservation of old people's independence and keeping them within 'the community'. But what do we mean by this? We cannot in all honesty describe hospital discharge to live alone and housebound as the preservation of independence and keeping an old person within the community. In such circumstances an old person is more cut off from the world than if he were living an institutionalized, but companionable, existence in an old folk's home. The term 'in the community' is bandied about in the loosest fashion and means no more than not being in a residential home or not being a patient in hospital. Similarly, the term 'preservation of independence' sounds more like a mere slogan than a useful aim for the social services to follow. How can we talk of the satisfactory preservation of independence when the old person concerned lives a lonely housebound existence, entirely dependent on the regular visits of a home help? And a classic contradiction in terms is made when we talk of preserving independence by the provision of more *sheltered* flatlet schemes.

In the context of this argument and in the light of Dr Nisbet's suggestion that many old people don't want to leave such institutions as hospitals, and that when they do relatives do not want them back, we must look again at exactly what we mean by living within the community and preserving independence.

What we must try to do is to see that old people live within *a* community; that within the limits of their frailties and disabilities they have the comfort and security of some form of community. At the same time their independence must be preserved as far as is possible, but let us also stop deluding ourselves that the provision of home helps and domiciliary services for lonely, housebound old people is, in every case, the proper preservation of independence. Many such old people would quite obviously be more a part of a community if they were living in a residential home.

Sheltered flatlets, despite the contradiction in terms, do provide a high degree of independent living and they, again, bring an old person into a community. Day centres too can help make an old person part of a community. These communities are not, generally, the wider community of the younger, active, working population and, on the evidence of the enjoyment of life in sheltered-flatlet schemes and the reluctance of some old people to leave the security of hospital, it is quite clear that many old people do not want to live in too close an association with the wider, active community.

Therefore, if old people are to live as they wish to live, within a community, and with the degree of independence compatible with their physical limitations, we need more residential homes and more sheltered-housing schemes. It is clear that in Sheffield at least the case for a massive new provision of places in residential homes has been made, and must be met quickly. The proper care of the elderly in Sheffield demands the security of this base from which to improve all other services for them.

Ten

Confused Elderly People
Living Alone

Although a Conservative Government was elected in June 1970 we remain a country committed towards the provision of social benefits from central and local government sources. Despite increasing prescription charges and tampering with housing subsidies, it is a measure of the change in our social philosophy that social welfare, social medicine and social housing are firm planks in the policy of Conservative as well as Labour Governments. While the methods and intensity of application may be different we have become, ineradicably, a socially-minded country in which the provision of social services must stay high on any government's order of priorities.

Perhaps the greatest shift in our thinking has taken place since the last war when, with the miseries of the 1930s, high unemployment, dole and means test consigned to history, and the austerity of wartime and the early post-war years behind us, the United Kingdom began to seek greater and more extensive social services for its people. Twenty years ago we would have considered the present range of services to be a marvellous achievement; yet it is symptomatic of our changed thinking that we are quick to criticize them when they are inadequate and hold the view that improvements are ours to demand by right. Indeed, we have that right, but criticism should be tempered with understanding of the problems the services face in extending themselves. Local authorities can only expand according to money they have available, the willingness of householders to see their rate poundage increased and the difficulties of attracting trained staff.

As Dr Clifford Shaw, Sheffield's Medical Officer of Health,

pointed out in the annual report on the Health of Sheffield for 1969, 'Most people care not one jot about the Os and Ms of how those services are provided. They are only concerned with the range and quality of the services and the readiness with which they are made available when needed.'

But, as we know, all local authority services concerned with the care of old people are in general overstrained and overworked. While the annual report on the Health of Sheffield does not gloss over the shortages and deficiencies, terse official language is far less expressive than that of a letter I received from a district nurse.

All the health and welfare services in Sheffield are desperately short of staff, particularly those caring for the elderly. As I write this, I am utterly exhausted following nine and a half hours on duty. I snatched half an hour for lunch from three to three-thirty p.m. (tea and sandwich while still wearing hat and coat). This is a frequent occurrence with many of my colleagues too, who also work for this department.

When we ask for more help in order to give more efficient care to those in need, we are told that this is impossible and infrequent adverts for staff very rarely bring forth suitable applicants. How can Sheffield Corporation increase services to the elderly if their present staff are leaving because they break under the strain and if personnel who retire, or leave for other reasons, are not replaced?

Despite the apparent strain from her work-load the writer of this letter was mistaken in her assumption that staff was not being increased and retiring or resigning personnel were not replaced. The Health Report shows, at the end of 1969, a day-duty nursing staff of 105 full-time and 13 part-time nurses, and that, although there were 19 resignations during the year, 30 new appointments were made. Similarly the night-nursing service, often used in terminal illness with the elderly constituting by far the largest number of users, had been steadily expanded since its introduction in 1966 and about eighty patients a month received this service.

The answer to her complaint is found in a description of the work-load.

A monthly average of five hundred new patients makes it imperative that the nursing staff concentrate on rehabilitation of the patient and indirectly also exhort relatives and friends to participate in this process. In every district nurse's case-load can be found a nucleus of chronic patients who have become psychologically as well as physically dependent on the service. The proportion of elderly in the community is on the increase and will necessitate the training of staff in a more positive approach towards this problem . . .

The increasing needs of the elderly in the community makes one very aware of gaps in the services, recognizing fully that other colleagues in the department have their limitations and planning problems. It is regrettable that chiropody service is not available for the housebound patient without a wait of many months. It is also questionable whether extra tasks such as fire-lighting and preparing breakfasts should be required of the trained nursing staff at weekends and Bank Holidays. To operate a five-day week rota of duties, nursing tasks have to be streamlined at week-ends. It would seem that the actual nursing tasks are receiving less attention than is desirable if nurses are asked to take work that is normally done on week days by the Home Help Service. These are points to be considered in future overall planning.

It is wasteful of the skill of a district nurse to have her perform menial household tasks because the Home Help Service does not operate at week-ends. The nurses obviously do not begrudge such work, but from the point of view of efficiency in an already overworked service this is not desirable.

But the Home Help Service in Sheffield also works under the handicap of having greater demands on its services than its numbers can provide. In 1969, a total of 2,873 requests for help were made and of these 2,130 were given assistance. The total number receiving the service in 1969 was 6,162.

The report said:

At the time there has been no increase in organizing or clerical staff and this considerable achievement reflects greatly to the credit of existing staff who have worked many hours beyond their normal duty. Regretfully it has had repercussions since quite understandably a few have felt unable to withstand the increasing pressures and volume of work. The Institute of Home Help Organizers recommend that the case-load of an organizer should not exceed two hundred patients but at the present time our organizers are dealing with over five hundred patients.

We should be quite clear that the home-help service is providing a great deal more than domestic services such as cleaning, cooking and fire-lighting. This section of the Health Report continues:

The increasing number of home helps have provided not only assistance to more patients, but also enabled us to provide more than a basic service in each home.

Confused elderly people, living alone, present complex problems in that their physical condition demands attention. Moreover, some live in conditions of squalor where the equipment available is very inadequate and this makes working conditions depressing and difficult. Even today many houses lack hot water supplies and still have old-fashioned Yorkshire ranges.

It is sometimes necessary to give an intensive service with a home help and a home warden calling at least twice a day. The helps attending these elderly patients become attached and genuinely fond of them, despite the problems they present.

During 1969 the number of home helps in Sheffield increased from 627 to 781 and the number of home wardens from 36 to 42 (24 more home wardens were budgeted for in the 1970 financial year). The report pointed out that ninety per cent of the people assisted by home helps received the service free of charge.

The Home Help and Home Warden Service also reported an anomaly brought about by the provision of more day hospital facilities.

An increasing number of patients are now attending day hospitals, and whilst this relieves the Home Help Service in some ways, it adds to its problems in others – the most difficult being the time factor. Generally the ambulance arrives by 9 a.m. but sometimes it is delayed and may not arrive before midday. In the latter case, if the patient is senile and confused, the help is unable to leave so her work with other patients is disrupted. Daily attendance at hospital does not always benefit the patient because of the upset and travelling involved, and sometimes they become tired and request a reduction or make excuses for not attending. On the other hand, when they are only attending two or three days in the week they do seem to derive benefit and look forward to the day out. As an incidental there is a reduction in the need for incontinent washing by the helps.

This section of the report gives an indication of the changes that have taken place in local authority social services when it says:

It is becoming increasingly obvious there are differing grades of responsibility in a home help's work, and different standards of work required to meet the varying social conditions, and different training schemes needed to equip the home helps with the knowledge and skills to meet all problems. It is essential to look beyond the flat hourly-paid system to make more realistic payment to the practical competent helps *who are tackling jobs far beyond the role of the domestic help visualized in the initial Health Act of 1946** There must be scope in the 1970s for the advancement of the home help herself if this service is to find the number and quality of staff it requires.

It notes too the growing demand for home wardens

due in great measure to the limited number of wardens, but also because old people are becoming much more conscious that they want and need someone calling regularly to ensure their safety and well-being. They need a reliable friend with whom they can discuss the numerous problems of old age, who can provide practical help and, when it is needed, understanding.

In services to the elderly Sheffield's health visitors almost doubled their activities in five years. The number of visits to old people rose from 8,762 in 1964 to 15,162 in 1969 But again this section of the Health Report commented on shortcomings. 'Preventive work in this field continues to be inadequate. There is an urgent need for more day assessment centres for the elderly with facilities for screening, counselling and health education.' (A new centre for this type of work was opened in 1970.)

During the year four full-time health visitors resigned and eight joined giving a year-end staff of fifty-three full-time and nine part-time visitors. The report noted the recently expressed

*Author's italics.

opinion of a team from the Department of Health that the number of health visitors should be increased to a hundred, and, in its final paragraph, the section referred to case-loads, many of which consist of well over a thousand families.

If health visitors are to give the specialized service for which their training prepares them they must have the present work-load reduced drastically and, if they are to provide a complete and comprehensive service, it is essential that clerical help should also be available to them.

To eliminate laborious clerical work it suggested providing each health visitor with a portable tape-recorder.

I have quoted earlier the staffing position of the Social Care Department at the end of 1969 and of its increased establishment of ten officers during 1970. But the difficulties of staffing become apparent with the knowledge towards the end of 1970 that turnover of staff had meant that the establishment had increased by only half the number budgeted for.

Thus, from these reports we can see quite clearly a position of increasing work, increasing staff and increasing expenditure; and also that provision of services is hardly keeping pace with demand. Thus the position of local-authority social services is invidious and the position of those who work for them unenviable. Quite obviously, with case-loads as high as those here recorded for Sheffield, the recruitment of staff is no easy task and, again, the big city finds itself at a disadvantage to areas of less social pressure.

These, and services to the handicapped, are the major domiciliary services provided for old people by local authorities and, while recognizing the devotion to duty of those who do the work, their long hours and the trying conditions under which they toil, the inadequacy of these services is amply demonstrated.

But despite this, local authority services have statutory duties of which the Seebohm Report gives a reminder when making out its case for organizational change:

Local authority personal social services are not fully meeting needs for which, on the basis of the duties placed on them by statutes, they are clearly responsible. Obvious examples can be derived from the waiting-lists for different kinds of day and residential care for the mentally ill, the mentally subnormal, the handicapped and the aged. There is no doubt also that in many areas domiciliary services like home helps or meals on wheels are falling short of meeting obvious needs which those in the service think they ought to be meeting.

Deficiencies of this nature have increasingly been highlighted by the research ... and comparative statistics ... which indicate considerable differences in the quantity of services provided in different areas. Such unevenness does not bear any systematic relationship to differences in local need.

Sheffield Corporation is clearly not fulfilling its statutory duty under the 1948 National Assistance Act to provide sufficient places in residential homes, if, on Seebohm's basis, the waiting-list is the ruling factor. One of the effects of not fulfilling this duty and of being slow off the mark in providing wardened sheltered-flatlet schemes is the obvious strain on every domiciliary social service which the Corporation provides.

This is not to say that these services would not be under stress in any case, but, had more residential homes and wardened flatlets been provided in the past, the strain would undoubtedly have been lessened. To what extent it is very difficult to estimate.

To return to the Health Report section on the Home Help Service, we find it speaking of confused elderly patients living alone whose physical condition demands attention. It also speaks of patients who need intensive care with helps and wardens calling at least twice a day. It speaks of them living in squalor without even hot water and of the helps waiting for ambulances with patients who are senile and confused.

Such is the state of our provision for old people that demonstrably the home-help service in Sheffield is caring for people who obviously need greater shelter than can be provided by domiciliary services in their own homes, who obviously in some cases could benefit from a place in a residential home or from living in wardened flatlet schemes. It is little wonder that this section should remark on home helps 'tackling jobs far beyond the role of the domestic help visualized in the initial Health Act of 1946'.

What must be questioned is whether the home help should be tackling jobs far beyond domestic work. While there is no alternative but for them to do such tasks as the present time, it is quite clear from this report that many of the old people who are assisted by home helps need greater shelter than is at present provided and, quite obviously, much readier access to skilled nursing.

All these services previously described, except Social Care, come under a local authority's health function. Social Care, which is responsible for the admission of old people to residential homes, is a separate entity. Sheltered, wardened flatlet schemes are the responsibility of the Housing Department but, of course, the warden's service is controlled by the Health Department. Sheffield's meals-on-wheels service is a joint effort between the Council of Social Service and the Health Department. The Council of Social Service provides the meals and volunteer helpers for the deliveries, the Corporation the vans and drivers. Similarly, there is a degree of separation in many functions which a Health Department exercises for old people.

While proper cooperation and coordination were expected to be claimed between these many activities, and indeed with the Housing Department as well, such interlocking of functions, especially with an overworked administration, must have been difficult to achieve.

One of the major arguments for organizational change put forward by the Seebohm Report was poor coordination.

Our knowledge and understanding of social need have steadily grown and this has underlined its complexity and the desirability of meeting it in a comprehensive fashion. In consequence the problems of coordination and collaboration within the personal social services, and between them and other services, have loomed increasingly large. The present structure of the personal social services and the division of responsibilities between them is based upon the definition of certain kinds of problems (mental illness, homelessness, or physical handicap, for instance); upon age groupings (the old, or school children), and upon legal and administrative classifications (delinquency or deemed maladjustment). Such divisions do not reflect the fact that families comprise members falling into a variety of these categories or that individuals may face a combination of inter-related problems for which different categories of services (or none) are responsible. Under these circumstances the growing desire to treat both the individual and the family as a whole and to see them in their wider social contexts creates accentuated difficulties of coordination both at policy and field levels.

Seebohm was commenting generally, but such strictures are equally applicable to services provided for old people. What in effect is being said is not that there was necessarily poor coordination between the services as then established, but that changing circumstances and the necessity of redefining need and seeing it in the context of the community made such collaboration as there was less meaningful and less effective. To make collaboration and coordination effective in the light of increasing knowledge and changing circumstances, organizational change in local authority social services was necessary.

Seebohm's major arguments for organizational change were inadequacies in the amount of provision, inadequacies in the range of provision, inadequacies in the quality of provision (all readily demonstrated), poor coordination, difficult access to the social services and insufficient adaptability.

On the latter point the Seebohm Report said:

The personal social services were not considered to be sufficiently adaptable to meet changes in the nature and extent of social need; a defect which was thought likely to be intensified in the future. Developing needs should be better foreseen, plans laid to meet them and the work adapted without undue stress or disruption ...

Such adaptability will be hard to achieve in a situation like that of Sheffield, where social services are hard pressed to discharge present duties, and particularly so since need is defined within the context of services at present available and redefining types of need will not only make demands on the machinery of coordination but will, very likely, increase the overall extent of provision which a local authority will have to make.

Then, again, there is divided responsibility, responsibilities which are divided not only between departments but within departments. The divisions under the previous health functions of health visitors, home nurses, home helps and services to the handicapped, are an example.

Seebohm said:

Staff in the separate departments are organized to achieve the specific objectives of those departments rather than to meet the full range of needs. This clearly militates against the prospect of helping a family or individual with multiple needs through a single worker or through a close-knit professional team with comprehensive responsibilities, since considerable time and energy are required to secure a common approach and avoid duplication.

Because of doubts about which service would provide certain forms of help or deal with certain kinds of problems it is sometimes difficult to ascribe responsibility for failure to any particular service, or to hold anyone accountable. Similarly, as we have already pointed out, the problems of accessibility and coordination are considerably aggravated by divided responsibility.

Seebohm built up a mountainous case for unified social service departments for local authorities and generally speaking the proposals, now effected by the Local Authority Social Services Act, 1970, were widely welcomed by officers and workers in these social services. Because a unified social service department will be bigger there will still be problems of coordination and it will be some time before any assessment can be made of how effectively these have been tackled.

Referring specifically to domiciliary services for old people, Seebohm spoke of the wide variety of help available but said, '... Cover differs considerably from place to place and nowhere do they assist more than a very small proportion of the old. Furthermore,' he went on, 'it appears that individual services have been started without sufficient thought for priorities or evidence of need over the whole area to be served. This piecemeal and haphazard development is unlikely to use scarce resources to the best advantage even though some assistance may be given to a fortunate few.'

Is such criticism applicable to social services provided in

Sheffield? The answer, I think, has to be yes, but at the same time we must remember that throughout the development of these services all have faced greater demands than they have been able to supply. Availability of staff in one section can lead to its progressing faster than another with greater staffing problems and certainly piecemeal, haphazard development can also be blamed on the previous division of responsibilities within a health and welfare department.

Seebohm's case is that a unified social service department will be able to take a more comprehensive view of the development of such services, but adds:

To do so it will have to know the extent and pattern of need in its area and be aware of all the local resources likely to be available. It will have to discover from local voluntary organizations what part they can play in providing a comprehensive service to the maximum number of old people. It will have to investigate fully the contribution which relatives, neighbours and the wider community can make and how the social service department can best enable such potential assistance to be realized. In this sense a considerable development of community care for the old may be achieved, even in the near future, by enlisting such help.

It would be unfair to suggest that local authorities such as Sheffield have not tried to take a comprehensive view in the past, But because they have not been able to achieve the quantity of provision required and have laboured to try to keep pace with increasing demands attempts to take the broader view and act upon it, they have been inhibited. Even so, the range and quantity of services they have been able to provide has been steadily expanded, year by year. But one of the commonest criticisms made of local authority social services as they existed until this year was that, having set up a home-help service, home nursing, chiropody service, services to the handicapped, etc., it then became necessary to define the needs of people within the individual scope of each of these services and that those with multiple problems obviously caused the services great difficulty. Furthermore, with case-loads as high as has been recorded, there must have been the temptation to only take on additional cases if they fell strictly within the limits of the service provided. In my view, further evidence of the inhibiting effect of these high case-loads is the emphasis which we found that the social services in Sheffield placed on some old people's refusal to be helped. Because of our own experience with old people during 1970 I have been constantly nagged by the feeling that what the social services call refusal – stressing that people have the right to refuse – was, in many cases, merely a reluctance which perseverance could have overcome.

Seebohm makes a similar point in talking about encouraging use of the social services: '... those who may require the help of the personal social services, for instance the welfare and children's services, encounter little encouragement to use them, nor is there a ready flow of simple information about their nature and how they can be obtained.'

Concrete confirmation of this came in Sheffield when *The Star* asked people who felt they were in need to contact the newspaper. Many people telephoned because they did not know what services were available to them and were satisfied when it was explained which might be able to help and were given addresses or telephone numbers.

By coincidence, while writing this section, I answered one such call. It was from a woman whose parents-in-law, aged seventy and seventy-four and not in the best of health themselves, were looking after a grandmother aged ninety-two, who had suffered from a stroke five days previously. The doctor had called daily and when they had tried to speak to the doctor about getting the grandmother into hospital he had not replied. My caller explained that her mother-in-law had hardly slept since the old woman's stroke and was annoyed that such old people should be expected to have the arduous task of nursing her grandmother. I explained that if they wished the old woman to be taken into a residential home she should contact the Social Care Department, but for immediate relief and to give her mother-in-law a rest she should speak to the Health Department in the hope that the night-nursing service would be made available. This situation illustrates that a number of things will have to be corrected if local-authority social services and, indeed, all other services connected with the welfare of the elderly, are to be made more efficient.

First of all, to take up Seebohm's point, there should be a ready flow of information about the services and how to use them. Secondly, why did the family doctor not tell the old people looking after the grandmother what local authority services were available to help them? Indeed, why did he not inform the Health Department himself? Better coordination than this between general practitioners and local-authority services will have to be achieved.

Seebohm continued the argument for encouraging use of the social services by saying:

Indeed, historically the aim has often been to deter people from seeking such help and stigma has attached to those who did. It is not surprising therefore that many are prejudiced against seeking the help of services they may need and to which they are entitled; indeed some remain ignorant of the purpose or even the existence of certain services ...

We can and should encourage those who need help to seek it. ... But if the structure remains complicated people will continue to be confused and hence often be deterred. One single department concerned with most aspects of 'welfare' as the public generally understands the term is an essential first step in making services more accessible. They must not be camouflaged by administrative complexity, or their precise responsibilities closely defined on the basis of twenty-year-old statutes ...

The unified social-service departments which Seebohm proposed and which have now been set up can, in my view, only lead to an improvement in local-authority social services. Co-ordination should be improved and, headed by a director of social services of equal rank in the local government hierarchy with a director of education, the status of social services will be improved. However, Seebohm's recommendations will only be successful if present case-loads are reduced by having extra staff to tackle them, so that the comprehensive, all-embracing view of welfare services can be taken. The present burden of work is such that to be effective many more workers will have to be recruited as well as making better use of the available voluntary services through better coordination with them. If more workers are to be employed by the personal social services conditions will have to be made more attractive. For example, to work in Sheffield as a social-welfare officer, considering the average case-load and taking into account a salary range of approximately £1,200 to £1,700 per annum, is not the most attractive proposition. It partly explains why there is the present turnover rate for staff.

It was in February 1970 that Alderman Mrs Patience Sheard, chairman of Sheffield's Health and Welfare Committee and later designated chairman of the Social Services Committee which would be its replacement, proposed that the City Council should pledge itself to finance and implement an overall plan for the development of all services for the elderly 'to such an extent that each retired person will have the right to decide for himself the manner in which he wishes to live'.

In the present circumstances of finance and staffing difficulties the implementation of Seebohm's recommendations – or indeed, fulfilling the duties of twenty-year-old statutes – to the extent required, and ultimately to the ideal proposed by Mrs Sheard, is going to be a long and difficult task.

In the upheaval which must come about with the setting up of unified social services departments such ideals must not be lost sight of in the complexities of reorganization and Mrs Sheard set the target for the old folk when she said : 'Just as we have a universal system for the education of children, so we ought to have a comprehensive system of service for the elderly.'

Eleven

Involving the Community

The success of any plans to make a better, richer life for the old people of this country must ultimately depend on the involvement of the community, the wider community which includes us all. The provision of social services, for which we pay out of rates and taxes, does not absolve us from personal responsibility.

Broadly speaking the aim of local authority personal social services is to provide domiciliary services for those who cannot help themselves. At the same time they should support the community which attempts to care for its old people. Thus, the totality of responsibility is not, and especially in the present circumstances of over-demand and staff shortages cannot lie, with the statutory services. Also, because statutory services define their functions within the limits laid down by Acts of Parliament, there are gaps which can only be filled by the work of individuals, relatives, friends and voluntary organizations.

Even though the Seebohm Report urged a reexamination of the definitions of need and an expansion of the range and variety of local-authority social services, it still said there would be increasing scope for voluntary organizations and community involvement.

At many points in this Report we have stressed that we see our proposals not simply in terms of organization but as embodying a wider conception of social service, directed to the well-being of the whole community and not only of social casualties, and seeing the community it serves as the basis of its authority, resources and effectiveness.

We tend to think of a community as those who live in a

particular district, area, estate or village, but such a definition is increasingly difficult to sustain, particularly in the urban environment of big cities where such long-established area or district communities are being uprooted and dispersed by slum clearance. A 'community' need no longer depend on neighbourhood. It can be a community of common interest created by education, by a place of work, by membership of the same social clubs or by membership of trade unions. Even so, planning for communities and attempts to create communities in new housing estates is usually based on the physical locality of groups of dwellings, and in most cases this traditional concept of community must hold good.

Most districts of Sheffield have some form of community or tenants' association. They vary widely in their aims and activities. Some, on the newer housing estates, have the use of impressive community halls and organize a wide range of social activities, including old folk's clubs. Others have sometimes channelled their activities into political agitation, such as in 1967 when they bitterly fought the Corporation's rent rebate scheme. Others, usually titled action groups, have been formed with the specific objects of presenting a united voice to either demand improved services from the Corporation or to scrutinize and modify Corporation plans for clearance and redevelopment in their areas. These action groups spring up in response to demands from people who feel their views are not breaking through the barriers of bureaucracy which surround town planning and slum clearance, but after they have completed the specific objectives of their formation they usually remain a watchdog of the public interest and retain their close ties with the community they serve.

Within the community of the whole city are many social and welfare organizations, some of which devote a considerable part of their activities to the welfare of the elderly. The most important is Sheffield Council of Social Service. This has sizeable premises in the city centre and a permanent staff as well as many voluntary workers. It provides a day-care centre and preparation for retirement courses and its old people's welfare committee coordinates some of the work for the elderly within Sheffield. It has two residential homes for the old, one of which provides a much-needed service as a half-way house between hospital and home and relieves families of sick relatives whilst they take holidays. A third provision is a group of self-contained flatlets. The Council of Social Services also provides Sheffield's meals-on-wheels service jointly with the Health Department. It has sponsored ninety-eight clubs for old people and a club for the old and disabled operates daily in its central premises. Furthermore, it gives training in social work for volunteers and social science students.

The Sheffield Churches' Committee for Community Care, an interdenominational body, operates 'good neighbour' schemes in several areas of Sheffield and the League of Good Samaritans also operates district-visiting and aid schemes to old and needy people in a number of areas. The Women's Royal Voluntary Service mostly concentrates its work on hospitals but still gives a fair amount of help to the elderly, including the provision of two blocks of bedsitters for old women. Other charities have provided old folk's homes. Churches also provide some services to the elderly in their parishes.

The organizations which set out to do active welfare work among the elderly are usually, like the statutory services, short of willing hands to help with the work. There are many other charitable and social organizations which could do work among old people or which could do more – the numerous women's organizations, for example. What they need is to be given proper encouragement and specific objectives within the areas they could serve. Active cooperation from the statutory services is also needed, accepting that voluntary organizations are responsible, in giving training and setting out objectives. The Council of Social Service, for example. because of its central, coordinating nature, achieves a reasonable degree of cooperation with the statutory services. But to some extent there appears to be a schism between the voluntary organizations and the local authority services. Many appear to have little faith in statutory provisions and one leading figure in voluntary work told. me they did not want to cooperate with the Corporation. They were disenchanted with the idea of involving themselves with Town Hall red tape.

Some interesting and telling information is contained in the first report of Sheffield's voluntary services liaison officer, who was appointed in February 1970. He circularized 320 voluntary organizations in Sheffield, asking the extent of their present work and the possibility of increasing it. Only 197 replied.

He pointed out that, in addition to the major voluntary organizations which I have already mentioned, such organizations as the Society of St Vincent de Paul, The Lions Club, Rotary and Round Table did limited amounts of work for the elderly. Old people are, of course, also assisted by such specialist organizations as the Royal Sheffield Institution for the Blind. Sheffield Corporation makes grants to 107 old people's clubs in the city, but, as this report points out, they cater mainly for those who are physically active.

The liaison officer was attempting to set up district organizations in forty small areas of the city and it soon became clear that this was to be a painstaking and slow task. In some areas he met enthusiasm from voluntary organizations which were already operating, in others apathy. In one area, for example, he arranged a meeting to which representatives of thirteen voluntary organizations had been invited. Only five turned up. Sometimes such preliminary meetings could not even be successfully arranged. Nor did he meet the enthusiasm he expected to encounter from clergymen, although there were exceptions. Apathy? Disinterest? Or a dislike of involvement with the Corporation? Perhaps a combination of all three.

His report pointed out that officers of the Health and Welfare Department had all agreed that there was a need and a place for volunteers to supplement the services which the Corporation provided.

It went on:

It is acknowledged that the field workers cannot cope with the pressures and the large case-loads they carry these days. It is obvious that one of the ways to ease this problem would be to use volunteers on a neighbourhood basis. If this need is to be met it will be necessary to get rid of the negative attitudes of both statutory workers and voluntary associations.

That indeed, is a remarkable admission, for until the report was issued in September the normal public practice of officials and councillors was to pretend that coordination was adequate and was being improved. And no one would have said that either volunteers or statutory workers held negative attitudes.

The passage continues:

Many voluntary bodies are imperfectly aware of their aims in any clearly formulated sense; these groups are characterized by an urge 'to do something'. They are aware of the existence of a problem and have a feeling that something must be done about it. As I see it the major need is to provide these people with objectives and some means whereby these objectives can be realized.

The report pointed out that the Corporation intended to employ a trained social worker whose duties would be directed to the training and preparation of volunteers for work in all fields where voluntary endeavour could effectively supplement the work of professional social workers.

In practice, the major effort would be directed towards meeting the needs of old people, since it is in this area that the problems are most immediate. Contact should be made between the local authority agencies and all voluntary organizations – good, bad and indifferent – with the object of providing support and 'something to offer' in return for their voluntary involvement.

The liaison officer suggested means of involving the community in work for the elderly:

Only by a system which involves all classes of people on a personal basis will it be possible to elicit the voluntary endeavours necessary for the effective community support of the aged. Put another way this means we must work at the grass roots in Sheffield: we must interest individuals whose previous experience of voluntary work has been disappointing. In short, we must have something to offer to be able to take volunteers through an induction course and give them appropriate training in the way in which they can be of maximum service and, *of equal importance, make them feel they are being of maximum service.**

This is a very valid point to make and the achievement of such an aim will be easier with the setting-up of small district groups in which volunteers will not only have a sense of being of maximum service but could have real responsibility. In my view they must be given such responsibility if they are to properly feel they are being of maximum service.

Why have previous attempts to enlist voluntary help failed? An answer was suggested in this report.

I think that in the past, attempts to enlist and operate voluntary workers in conjunction with local authority welfare workers have failed for psychological reasons. The professionals, even when inspired by goodwill, have tended not to let volunteers do very much, and some have been discouraging. Voluntary work must yield some satisfaction to the volunteer. In the past volunteers have not had this satisfaction since the tasks, when allotted by social workers, have been small and undemanding.

I am not implying that volunteers can undertake the same responsibility as social workers, but many volunteers are capable of much more than 'fetch and carry' work, and must be given the training commensurate with their capabilities.

The problem which faces the new social service departments is to get rid of such negative attitudes and give proper responsibilities to voluntary bodies, so that their services can be fully effective. However, if voluntary organizations are to continue to view the local authority as an agency to be avoided there is little chance of worthwhile cooperation being achieved. Like local-authority social services, voluntary organizations should conduct an examination of their aims and their resources to see whether they are making the best use of their capabilities in the light of the needs of the community they serve. Some, of course, are already efficient; I would not, for example, suggest that Sheffield's Council of Social Service is not doing all it is capable of doing and not channelling its effort in the right directions. But many other organizations who could help, or who could be more precise about what they want to do, need to take stock

*Author's italics.

of their function in the light of the social changes around us. Nor would I excuse voluntary organizations from a degree of arrogance in their rejection of cooperation with the local authority – their assumption that they know better. Indeed, during 1970 in Sheffield, with a few bright exceptions, I was not particularly impressed by the work of voluntary organizations. Furthermore, a campaign which ran for a year provoked surprisingly little comment from local churches, in particular from the leaders of the churches, with one notable exception. It is quite clear that the community leadership which was once ascribed to the churches in their parishes is no longer to be found and that in involving the community in the care of the elderly focal points other than parish churches must be found. Denominational difference, despite such activities as the 'good neighbour' scheme, remain a divisive influence in the community and the unfortunate tradition that the churches are only interested in those of their own persuasion persists. On one occasion I was telephoned by a parish priest who wished to pass over responsibility for handling the problems of a woman because 'she's not one of mine'. The woman and her young family could have benefited from the advice and assistance of the local-authority services, but the priest was unaware of what those services were and where they could be contacted. From the attitude adopted and the disinterest shown in social problems by some clergymen, it is not surprising that churches now have little influence in the community. They should realize that they are not dealing with problems which can be solved by pious exhortation but with problems which demand active participation and leadership from them. It is surprising that the churches have not taken a much more positive attitude over the challenging community and social problems of the day for in this could lie the restoration of their authority and influence.

In the past few years social changes within the geographical communities of large urban areas have been many and far-reaching in their consequences. Only now are we beginning to properly appreciate what slum clearance and redevelopment have meant to our communities. In Sheffield, with 40,000 new homes since the war and an impressive record of slum clearance, whole communities have been dispossessed and relocated. Action groups as watchdogs for this process are a fairly recent phenomena. People are becoming increasingly aware that such vast changes in the structure of their communities can have detrimental effects on their lives and they are becoming more vociferous in opposition when they think that the planners are wrong. Perhaps the most unfortunate effect of slum clearance is the planning blight which spreads throughout a neighbourhood which is scheduled to be destroyed. Sheffield has many such areas of, generally, two-up two-down houses in a state of rapid deterioration. Apart from lacking bathrooms and inside lavatories some are without hot-water systems and, because large numbers are owned by private landlords who receive minimal rents from them, maintenance work to prevent rising damp and leaky roofs has often not been carried out. In view of the level of rents and the imminence of demolition landlords cannot be expected to carry out fairly simple repairs which would cost them as much as a year's rent. There are some well-known slum landlords in Sheffield who deliberately make themselves unavailable to their complaining tenants and the sooner the slums they own have been compulsorily purchased by the Corporation the better.

An example of the difficulties such landlords can create occurred when the Corporation wished to demolish and rehouse families living in a group of the most deplorable slums where walls were running with damp. Although rents were still being collected by agents, the Corporation was unable to break through the screen surounding the landlord to find out who he was so that notice to treat, for the compensation to be paid, could be served on him. Eventually, because of the desperate condition of the families living in these slums, the Corporation served them notice of entry, rehoused them and went ahead with demolition, thus leaving itself open to action for compensation in the Lands Tribunal. By creating such difficulties the landlord was delaying the time when he would stop receiving rents. Most families in these situations are too poor to rehouse themselves and they look to the Corporation for protection and shelter.

Population changes take place in a clearance area in the years preceding demolition. Some of those who can afford to do so move out and the houses they vacate are often reoccupied by Commonwealth immigrants. Thus in Sheffield, as in most other towns and cities, we find that the main concentrations of Commonwealth immigrants live in redevelopment areas. This in itself causes a change in the character of the community. Many of these immigrants will themselves seek to move out when they have saved sufficient money to buy their own homes. But one of the results of the changes which take place in clearance area communities is that, because they are the poorest section of the population with no chance of improving their financial position, a large number of those who have to be rehoused from slum clearance are elderly.

The middle-aged and the elderly can be seen as the most stable elements of a slum clearance community, but we should not be led to the mistaken view that they always wish to retain that changed community which planning blight has thrust upon them. They are frequently glad to leave their inadequate homes and often state preferences for rehousing which scatter them throughout the suburban housing estates. Therefore we should not blame the local authorities for the community dispersal which takes place with slum clearance, particularly when the elderly among them wish to be rehoused near their families where this is possible. What the local authority does, however, is to try to rehouse the bulk of those from a slum-clearance community on the same, or a neighbouring, new estate in an attempt to make the creation of a new community easier. But there are still many who question what the local authority tries to do, especially when slum clearance means rehousing on a windy, hilltop estate, a long bus ride from the city centre. What people object to, especially the old, is dispersal which takes them a long way from the city. They find it incomprehensible that the planners wish to rehouse them on the outskirts and the question is constantly posed: 'Why don't they build more flats and houses near the centre?' Sheffield has, in fact built a great many new homes within walking distance of its centre, but claims that the land is not available to do more. In my view it could take a closer look at the availability of land near the centre and make greater efforts towards redevelopments which will rehouse people in the same district as the one from which they have been dispossessed, thus preserving something of the old community in a geographical as well as in a social sense.

In the past slum clearance has been too concerned with the bricks and mortar, the availability of building land and the mechanics of moving people, without giving sufficient examination to the sociological changes which would take place. The people dispossessed have had far too little opportunity to make known their feelings and to influence the course of events which the planners have decreed. Therefore the emergence of vigorous, vociferous action groups is a welcome sign. They must refuse to be ignored by those with political power and must refuse to accept the stock answer that decisions have been made which cannot be altered. It is encouraging that these organizations are usually deeply concerned with the elderly people they represent, but the irony is that they generate a new sense of community at a time when that community is about to be dispersed.

From the distress and loneliness of many old people it is quite clear that community development both on new estates and in old districts must be further encouraged on a wide scale. Here again we see no consistent pattern of service. Some communities provide good facilities for their old people, others provide little. Some areas have a deep sense of community, others hardly any.

The Seebohm Report said:

There are many benefits to be gained for individuals and families from a sense of belonging to a community and of participating in its various common activities, and the development of this identity and activity is important in securing an effective family service. The term 'community development' is used primarily to denote work with neighbourhood groups. Community development in this country is seen as a process whereby local groups are assisted to clarify and express their needs and objectives and to take collective action to attempt to meet them. It emphasizes the involvement of the people themselves in determining and meeting their own needs. The role of the community worker is that of a source of information and expertise, a stimulator, a catalyst and an encourager.

The problem is the involvement of enough people. As we have seen from the approaches Sheffield's liaison officer made to voluntary organizations and to local communities, there does not seem to be a vast surplus of voluntary resources available to be used.

As Dr Clifford Shaw pointed out in his 1969 annual report on the Health of Sheffield:

The problem of the old and the infirm looms as a spectre which the health and welfare services are powerless to combat without the goodwill and material aid given by relatives, neighbours and through voluntary associations. In some areas of the City a community spirit of self-help has existed for many years and in others it has been established more recently through active community associations. But people like to help through a personal sense of responsibility felt for an individual and it would be unrealistic to imagine there is a large pool of untapped volunteers waiting to step forward at the first roll of the drums.

In my view the Corporation could make a much bigger effort to attract volunteer help and to coordinate it than it has done so far. We must remember that throughout 1970 *The Star* published many stories about the distress of old people and about those who gave help yet, despite the difficulties the liaison officer was encountering, the chief officials of the Health and Welfare Department never sought the assistance of the local press to appeal for volunteers. Meanwhile through its Women's Circle (a magazine feature for its women readers) the paper managed to set up a number of district groups of housewives to visit old and lonely people in their areas. The Seebohm Report took the view that the proper agency for promoting community activity was the new Social Service Department.

Community identity can be encouraged indirectly by the creation and development of the appropriate social and physical environment and here the social service department should be involved in social planning, acting in concert with, for example, housing, planning and other departments of local and central government concerned with new towns, schemes for urban renewal and other developments which affect the community environment. Community identity may also be developed through organizations such as community centres, clubs, play centres and tenants' associations where the social service department could provide technical and professional help, information, stimulation and grant-aid.

A clear responsibility then should be placed upon the social-service department for developing conditions favourable to community identity and activity. Just as we have argued that the family often needs assistance and encouragement to perform many of its mutual aid and caring functions, so too the wider groups to which people belong need help in developing these attributes. We are not suggesting that 'welfare through community' is an alternative to the social services but that it is complementary and inextricably interwoven.

While I would agree that voluntary and statutory social work are inextricably interwoven, Seebohm is being somewhat idealistic in saying that social-service departments have the duty of stimulating community development. In view of the present staffing position in social-service departments and the upheaval which their setting up will have caused in many areas it is perhaps unrealistic to suggest they will have the time, manpower and money to act as a decisive spur to building new communities for some time to come. And, indeed, when they are able to give considered encouragement on the basis of social knowledge of all aspects of life in a community, the real drive for community identity and development must come from within the community itself, with volunteers holding real and satisfying responsibility.

Communities, whether stable and old established or new and developing, should look for greater participation in the services which the local authority, and for that matter voluntary bodies, provide them. I have already remarked on the frustration of many people in Sheffield in their approaches to the local authority and better consultative machinery will have to be set up. The need to form action groups and to take their troubles to newspapers in the hope that publicity will produce results is proof enough that people are not consulted as much as is necessary.

Seebohm said:

Implicit in the idea of a community-oriented family service is a belief in the importance of the maximum participation of individuals and groups in the community in the planning, organization and provision of the social services. This view rests not only upon the working-out of democratic ideas at the local level, but relates to the identification of need, the exposure of defects in the services and the mobilization of new resources. The consumer of the personal social services has limited choice among services and thus needs special opportunities to participate.

At the moment those opportunities are not properly available and, as Seebohm points out, citizen participation not only provides a source of information about need and a pool of manpower to help the services, but also means by which consumer control can be exercised over professional and bureaucratic power.

Does the community really care about the social problems in its midst? I believe that it does, once it knows what the problems are and ways of tackling the problems are pointed out. People need to care more deeply about the suffering of the elderly, not just those who are personally touched through friends or relatives, but the community as a whole. When more people are made thoroughly aware of the crying needs within their midst more voluntary help will be forthcoming and communities, through their various organizations and associations, will seek to provide and encourage better services for the aged, just as a number did in Sheffield as a result of press publicity.

But I also think that in part the present situation is due to the lack of explicit, widely publicized warnings in the past by the authorities in general. The provision of widespread statutory social services has misled people into the belief that these services will take responsibility and that they are capable of dealing with all the problems that arise. This is not so and people should not think that personal responsibility can be handed over to the local authority.

Seebohm said:

It is not surprising that the reaction to the increased government responsibility for health, welfare and education is to assume that there is less need for voluntary service. This is not the case. With the continuing growth of the personal social services it will be more necessary for local authorities to enlist the services of large numbers of volunteers to complement the teams of professional workers, and the social-service department must become a focal point to which those who wish to help can offer their services.

Sheffield could have taken much more urgent action than it has done to improve liaison with voluntary workers and individuals, but, as I pointed out in an earlier chapter, this opportunity was missed at a time early in 1970 when the public conscience on the subject of old age was most aroused.

Despite all the efforts of 1970 the coordination of work within the community as a whole remains a task which must have firm objectives and strong central direction if it is to be achieved.

Twelve

Poverty and
Social Justice

The old-age pension in 1970 was £5 for a single person and £8 2s. for a married couple. On any view of them they are miserably inadequate and totally indefensible figures. Which of us could live on this income? Which of us could even exist on it? But this is what we say is sufficient for about eight million people.

Even with supplementary benefits to pay for rents, is £5 a week anything like enough to pay for food, fuel and light at today's prices? It is not even a question which needs arguing. We have only to look at our own weekly budgets, then prune them to the barest essentials, to realize that it is not sufficient.

Nor has it been for many years. The prospect of retirement holds no attraction. Those who had savings when they retired have seen them gradually eroded as the cost of living increased and the financially stable old age they planned has crumbled about them. It is all very well for men like Mr Jack Jones, leader of the Transport and General Workers' Union, to speak as he did in December 1970 of the Tory Government's 'callous indifference to the needs of the pensioners', or for Mr Vic Feather, general secretary of the Trades Union Congress, to tell the same meeting 'If you could come out on strike for increased pensions I would bloody well lead you.' That is to make it seem as if the election of Mr Edward Heath was the moment when pensions became criminally low. We all know that the old-age pension was entirely inadequate under the previous Wilson Governments and the Conservative Governments before them. Living in poverty or near poverty, they must have been hurt and angry when Harold Macmillan was telling the country 'you've never had it so good'.

For more than ten years now the old-age pension has meant living on the breadline and succeeding Governments can all be blamed for failing to give the old a proper income. Pension increases have always been granted to catch up with prices that have already increased, not to meet needs as they have arisen. Despite all the economic ills which have frustrated the country in recent years we remain one of the rich nations of the world. But the share of our wealth which we give to the old, be it in pensions, housing and social services, is not nearly a big enough proportion of the whole. This is a sad commentary on the failure of capitalist economics and on the fiscal policies of the allegedly Socialist Government of 1964 to June 1970. The Labour Party certainly failed to give old people a better deal and there is a stink of hypocrisy when its politicians now attack the Heath administration for the same failing.

But at least, when she spoke at a Labour rally in the Albert Hall in December 1970, Mrs Shirley Williams, Labour spokesman on Health and Social Security, acknowledged that we had reason to feel ashamed and provided some interesting comparisons in the course of her speech.

Many people in Britain do not realize how wide the gap is between pensions in this country and in other countries with a similar level of economic development. A man in Britain, earning £25 a week, who has contributed all his working life will get £5 plus 13s. 6d. graduated pension. But a man earning the equivalent amount would get £9 in Holland, £10 in the USA and £19 in Australia or Italy. Even in poverty-stricken Portugal he would do better than in Britain.

Although Mrs Williams was not reported as giving the comparative rates of contribution, even if one assumes that they are higher than in this country this is proof that other countries have overtaken the United Kingdom in the provision of social benefits. Indeed, we have clung to the myth that our health and welfare services and social-benefits systems were the best and most rewarding in the world for far too long.

Mrs Williams pointed out that the cost of living was going up by more than seven per cent a year or 1s. 6d. in the pound.

At that rate the whole of the November 1970 increase in supplementary benefits would have disappeared within a month. A question in Parliament on 26 November 1970 brought the information that by November 1971 the pension would be worth 14s. 5d. less in a year – lower in purchasing power than at any time since 1965. Mrs Williams, of course, could not resist making the point that the amount given back to the taxpayers by the Conservative reduction of 6d. on the standard rate of income tax was the equivalent of giving pensioners £1 a week rise, or about £350,000,000 in a year.

On a pension of a mere £5 a week a reduction in its buying power of 14s. 5d. is more than serious; it is insupportable. It leaves them in the position described by Mr Des Wilson, the director of Shelter, when he visited Sheffield in October. 'Already old people who get only £5 a week to live on have to choose between heating and eating and the least we should do is provide them with enough to survive on during the winter. To keep old people below the poverty line is totally unnecessary and we should carry them throughout their last years,' he said.

Unfortunately, although the Conservative Government rushed through legislation to pay pensions to the previously excluded over-eighty-year-olds, at the time of writing (December 1970) no increase had been generally granted to combat the rigours of winter and to protect old people's food and fuel supplies.

Professor Peter Townsend, chairman of the Child Poverty Action Group, has defined poverty as 'conditions which deprive people of those diets, those customs, those holidays, which everybody. else can enjoy'. Having looked at the poverty of the elderly in Sheffield in 1970 I would say a much harsher description of their poverty should apply than that given by Professor Townsend. He was attempting to define a line at which poverty begins, but thousands of old people live well below that line. Throughout 1970 it became increasingly clear that raging inflation was making life more and more difficult for old people and they were threatened by crushing poverty, increasing malnutrition and death from cold.

In my view the leaders of our country have shirked the problem of old age poverty for years and it is a matter which should be shirked no longer. When there are increases in the price of essentials – food, fuel, gas and electricity – then proportionate pension increases should be given automatically and not be delayed until the old folk's standard of poverty has suffered. In 1971 price rises were forecast for both gas and electricity, but we heard nothing about how such blows were to be made easier for the elderly.

Many suggestions can be made for making life financially easier for old people. Sheffield was one of the first of the towns and the cities which give off-peak free travel to pensioners. This affords them some saving and raises the question of whether we should give them free travel on buses everywhere and at all times. There is also strong support for the idea of letting old people have television and radio licences for a nominal price. Making television available to old people, either through special cheap rentals or through cheap licences, would be a blessing for many. We encountered numerous old people who could not afford the licence fee and to pay for rentals (say about 9s. 6d. a week) or repairs, was often more than many others could afford. In recognition of the poverty of old people almost every place of public entertainment offers them concessionary rates, just as they do for children, and this is another way of helping the old to afford their outside interests.

But is this what old people want and need? Surely it would be better for them if they did not have to campaign for the charity of cheap television licences and if they did not have to depend on the charity of reduced prices for OAPs? Would it not be a boost to their feelings of independence and a retention of their pride if they could afford to pay like the rest of us? Old people do not take kindly to charity. This is amply proved by their reluctance to claim supplementary benefits, which so many of them refer to as charity and still refuse to accept. Independence is what keeps them struggling against the adversities of life, acceptance of charity merely wears them down.

At present-day prices it would take a big increase in pensions to give even a glimmer of social justice to old people. If £1 a week increase costs the country £350,000,000 a year, can we afford to give the kind of pension increase which is necessary if old people are to be properly fed, properly warmed and are to enjoy the benefits of life which the rest of us too often take for granted? No doubt esoteric economic arguments can be produced to show how little an increase need be or how little the country can afford, but we have a duty to manage the economy in a way which will make such an increase possible and will provide sufficient funds for the other social services old people need.

It would be an optimistic man who would expect such a duty to be discharged by a Conservative Government, committed as it is to Capitalistic policies. A reduction in the standard rate of income tax, even of only 6d. in the pound – a major benefit only to the better-off – was a sign of what might be to come. Similarly we have been given all the usual Tory pronouncements of 'letting prices find their own level', of a 'free' economy and of an emphasis on 'free' enterprise, policies which in no capitalist country in the world benefit the poor and those on small fixed incomes. What we have not heard since the General Election is the promised Tory plans for dealing with rising prices, a matter which Mr Heath claimed he could settle 'at a stroke'.

As expected, the Tory plan for dealing with rising prices is first to blame all rising prices on wage increases and then to try to thwart trade union demands at every turn. They (both the Chancellor of the Exchequer, Mr Anthony Barber and Mr Robert Carr, Minister for Employment) have warned the country that wage rises *must* be followed by price rises.

This is the inexorable logic of capitalism – that private profits must be maintained – and it takes no account of the low-paid and those on fixed incomes who will be hurt in the process. The only way in which a Government can achieve a genuine accord with trade unions is to give them reason for modifying wage demands by clamping down on price-rises. Clearly, the present Government does not intend to do this and so risks worsening relations with the TUC and even more industrial strife if its Industrial Relations Bill becomes law in its published form. There is little chance of industrial peace in this country – the peace that will benefit those who are unable to help themselves and have no militant voices to plead their causes – until radical new policies have achieved a much fairer distribution of the wealth of this country. Failure to do this by the previous Labour Government and failure to prevent rising prices at a time when wages were held down meant that instead of redistribution the poor became poorer and the rich became richer, the gap between them widening all the time. Present policies of the Tory Government do not lead one to think that the trend will be reversed. It is now an acknowledged fact that poverty – not just among the most helpless, the elderly, but among families as well – has become a serious problem in the United Kingdom and I would agree with Professor Townsend that the proposed Families Income Supplement is not the real answer, but merely another expedient, a political sop in the maintenance of an unjust system.

No doubt the present Government will award increases in the old-age pension, and like Labour and Tory Governments before them, impress the country with their false magnanimity. They may even truly believe they are being generous when they do so. But I have no doubt that any increase Mr Heath's Government makes in old-age pensions will be insufficient to give old-age pensioners a decent standard of living and a proper degree of independence. Such increases will always follow prices which have already risen – just as they have done in the past.

I am not optimistic about the future for old people if they have to depend on State pensions under present governments. We would be foolish to believe that pensioners will even get social justice in this area as long as governments are committed to upholding the 'right' of individuals to make private profit at the expense of their fellow men. Pensioners retire poor ; they have worked all their lives to make others rich. In retirement they are poverty-stricken, the due reward of their old age denied them by the need to uphold a capitalist system which feeds on the labour of the people. Only when the wealth of the country, in all its aspects, is used for the benefit of all the people, when there is an end to the selfishness of big business and there is no longer a legally protected 'right' to profit from the labours of our fellow men, only then will we be able to plan an economy which will give social justice to old people.

Thirteen

Only Those Eligible
to be Helped

In condemning society for its present and past failure to care for the elderly, to give them the kind of houses and communities they need, to provide adequate medical services and a sufficiently numerous domiciliary service in their own homes, we must ask what has been the root cause of that failure. At the bottom of it is our lack of knowledge of the extent of the variety of problems and the numbers who need help. Nor do we know, despite the Registrar General's population projections, how many more will need help in future. Future planning is very largely guesswork based on the present extent of known need. As we learned in Sheffield in 1970 there were many old people with a wide variety of needs whose existence was unknown to the social services or the voluntary organizations who could help them, all adding to the extent of known need and, presumably affecting future projections.

But without precise knowledge, future plans will not provide the best service, or indeed the type of service which may be required. The best that can be said about all provisions for old people is what Seebohm said about housing them: 'Little attempt has been made to estimate the total need ... but it is clear that need greatly exceeds supply.'

It is fair to assume that the extent and variety of problems in big cities and towns will be roughly the same in proportion to population. But, as we have already seen, some towns and cities have made more progress in one direction (e.g. old folk's homes) than others, while some rural areas have made better total provision. Therefore, with a wide variation of provision, and in some cases population distribution, future needs will have to be investigated on a local basis to fit local circumstances.

There can be no ignoring the fact that this is an enormous task. We need to know how many old people live in any particular area, how old they are, whether they live alone, what is their state of health and how it affects their lives, whether they receive adequate help from children or relatives and whether that help will continue, whether they receive no help, and if not, what assistance they need from the statutory services or from voluntary organizations. We need to inquire into the full circumstances of all old people who are likely to be uprooted by slum clearance to determine in to what sort of accommodation they need, and wish, to be rehoused. We need to inquire into how closely they are involved with a community and find out how closer involvement can be achieved. And above all we need to know which of them are at risk and why.

In 1968 the Seebohm Report advocated the setting-up of research and intelligence units.

More effective personal social services mean making better decisions about how to assist individuals and families, and better decisions depend upon better information ...

In the past there has been little real planning in the personal social services and this has had unfortunate effects. Some of the problems we saw and heard about appeared to have been aggravated because they had not been foreseen, though they surely could have been, and because in consequence arrangements to deal with them had been made too late. The planning of the personal social services cannot be undertaken successfully without the research which identifies emerging trends, assesses long-term repercussions, and estimates the character and dimension of future needs.

We consider the general case for research to be undeniable. That it frequently has a disturbing impact is no argument against it. Indeed, it represents one important insurance against complacency and stagnation. Greater knowledge of the problems facing the personal social services could help to clear away the fogs of optimism and pessimism which are apt to afflict those responsible for them; by optimism we mean the view that if sufficient money is put into the services as they are now they will automatically improve; by pessimism we mean the view that in the present state of ignorance about social problems and how to resolve them, it is not possible to do much to make the personal social services more effective.

Sheffield's research and intelligence unit, serving all Corporation departments, was established in 1970 and was directed by resolution of the City Council on 4 February to ascertain the needs of the elderly and whereby those needs could be fulfilled.

On 24 September it produced a preliminary report saying how it intended to fulfil the terms of that directive and I was not surprised when the report stressed the difficulties that had to be faced. Our own investigations, as well as bringing to light new cases, also showed the complexity of many cases, and variety in the types of need was often encountered in the circumstances of one old person.

Not only are great problems present in assessing the type of need in a manner in which it can be statistically expressed, but there are also great problems in discovering cases of need.

Some local authorities, again usually the smaller ones, have compiled lists of pensioners, but this is not as easy to do as it sounds. It needs coordination between the present records of Health and Welfare Departments, between National Health Service Executive Councils and the Supplementary Benefits Commission, who are the most likely agencies to have records of needy old people. Even so, such a compilation would not reveal every needy old person in any particular area and would not reveal the accurate extent of need in every case. Electoral rolls, because they do not reveal the age of the person involved, are no use for this purpose.

In some areas there have been house-to-house surveys, sometimes with the aid of voluntary organizations, but this too has its drawbacks. Such a survey could discover information regarding which old people live alone and may say how many *appear* to be in need of help, but some follow-up assessments by a trained social worker and/or health visitor would be necessary to give precise information about their condition, the extent of their need and the services they require. Old people often give plaintively inaccurate information about themselves and finding the truth can be a time-consuming business. 'Nobody ever comes near. I'm on my own all the time,' says the old woman. But inquiries from the neighbours will discover that they call regularly and help with shopping and housework and that a relative visited only a matter of days previously.

But this kind of survey only assesses the present need; the task becomes even more perplexing and complicated when one attempts to discover the potential cases and apply preventive measures before serious deterioration in either the physical or mental condition of an old person has taken firm hold.

Seebohm said:

It is not for us to set out in detail for local authorities how they should identify and assess need, but we are certain that unless they can evolve a system of early detection which is suited to local circumstances they will be unable to provide an adequate overall service for the old.

This will require cooperation and understanding at all levels in the whole community as well as a definite place known to all to which anyone in need can be referred with the certain knowledge that appropriate action will be taken where necessary.

He made a similar point in an earlier paragraph:

... There are enough potential applicants for help to keep the detection services continually at full stretch. And where need has been discovered it must be met if the confidence of old people is to be retained in future.

Unfortunately at the present time many people, including the elderly, lack confidence in the social services. We received many complaints that where such services as home helps had been applied for they did not arrive for sometimes weeks after application and often visits were not frequent enough for the old people concerned. Requests for visits from social workers sometimes met slow response, and requests for much-needed warden services could not be met.

We know full well that the reasons for these failures are over-work and inability to recruit sufficient staff but such logical explanations fall on deaf ears when people firmly believe that the case they refer to the social services is of the most urgent (whether it is or not).

The preliminary report of Sheffield's Research and Intelligence Unit recognized all these difficulties, but made curious references to minorities: 'This report is mainly concerned with the last group of "unmet need". Most surveys suggest this is a significant, but small, *minority** of old people,' and again: 'There is also the formidable professional problem of screening all old people who are willing to be helped to find the *minority** in need of a particular service.'

But the same report pointed to the fact that over three hundred elderly Sheffield people were in urgent need of places in old folk's homes – a number nearly half as many as the total places – a hundred urgently needed home helps and 1,200 needed more assistance from home helps. This of course is known need, but it is also unmet need. We also know, without any doubt, that the demand for old people's housing far exceeds supply, that services generally are inadequate and that it has been estimated that a very large number of old people are in need of psychogeriatric care. All this would suggest that, while those old people who require the help of statutory or voluntary services are a minority of the total elderly population, their numbers are very considerable and that to refer to them as minorities, or even small but significant minorities, is somewhat misleading.

Certainly, the report, in its appendices giving general conclusions from a study of surveys already undertaken, contradicts itself by saying: 'The proportion of over sixty-fives and especially over seventy-fives who have some sort of medical or social problems is probably substantial. Although the proportion who need local authority services may not be large, the numbers of people who appear to be in need, even on a fairly restricted definition, vastly exceeds the numbers receiving help.'

I found this contradictory reference to minorities disturbing, particularly the second reference in the main body of the report which made a fact of the suggested minority of the first reference. In my view no Research and Intelligence Unit should

Author's italics.

164

start a survey on the welfare of the elderly by making such a broad and dangerous assumption if it intends to provide the information on which correct future policies can be based.

This report also talks about eligibility and willingness to be helped. My view is that such considerations should be excluded from any accurate survey. Even if an old person is ineligible or unwilling to be helped by local authority services the survey should record such cases.

But a blanket survey of every old person in a city as big as Sheffield would appear to be impossible for local authority alone without a big outlay of manpower and expense. 'To visit all old people in the city once a year, allowing an average of fifteen minutes per person, would give full-time employment to about twelve people and it is unlikely that such a rigid schedule could be met or would be sufficient to give adequate diagnosis of need for those who are willing to accept it.'

The report goes on to suggest that one way of cutting down the expense was to concentrate on particular parts of the city where the number of old people or the need was thought to be greatest. 'This still means contacting many old people not in need or who would not welcome help and would still fail to identify unmet need elsewhere . . .'

The report defined four types of unmet need, those 'eligible but not helped', those 'inadequately helped', 'fringe cases', where the help needed might be very little, and 'unknown problem' cases which no particular service set out to solve.

The report said :

There is little information about the third category of 'fringe' cases. The size of this category depends very much on decisions about what level of severity of need should be met by the services. Once those who are 'eligible but not helped' are covered the further the services are expanded the less severe in general the need dealt with at each level of expansion. There are no existing surveys of local authority services that are up-to-date or thorough enough to provide this information. Any advance in knowledge in this direction requires painstaking work on how to measure the levels of need and it is recommended that the Unit looks further at this question.

With the fourth category of 'unknown problem' cases there is the same lack of information. The difficulty, however, is somewhat different as it involves recognizing and measuring problems (for instance to do with low incomes) which Town Hall services are for historical, statutory and financial reasons not equipped to tackle. By its nature it is an unknown quantity and would require a wide-ranging survey.

After recommending that such a survey should be undertaken the report says that the survey would be beyond the resources of the Research and Intelligence Unit if other existing work was to continue and therefore, and because its results would be useful to other organizations, other bodies should be asked to contribute to its cost.

To my mind this would be the most important part of the survey and, to give credit to the report, it recognizes that the conclusions could suggest changes in the scope of existing services and also be relevant to coordination with outside voluntary bodies. Conclusions could also be very relevant to coordination with the family doctor services and the National Health Service.

Further criticisms of this report can, however, be made, first for its naïvety and secondly for its proposal on the 'best approach' to identify need.

'More information is wanted on why old people in need are not coming forward and a study of the reasons for this is recommended,' it says. This is fairly simply answered. Most of them do not come forward for fear of involvement with 'the authorities' or because they expect that nothing would be done if they did identify themselves.

Having dismissed earlier a 'door-knocking' survey, this report concludes that the best approach to identification 'seems to be through publicity. It has several advantages.' These 'advantages' are listed as excluding old people not in need or who would not welcome help; overcoming resentment of 'being on a list'; and, because much need was sudden and urgent, publicity rather than irregular screening was more likely to put people in touch with services when they wanted them.

Already this proposed survey is busily reducing its depth and its scope. It has already shown itself to be concerned only with those who will be eligible for local authority services and now it wants, even welcomes, methods of investigation which will exclude those who do not ask for help, but who, very often, are those in most need of help and whom persuasion can assist. Such people, and many more, would be unlikely to be identified by publicity.

Having talked of the advantages of publicity the report then produces another grand contradiction. 'Publicity, or any method of identifying need, will inevitably increase the demand on services. Part of the new demand (the worst cases of those "eligible but not helped") may be substituted for those in less urgent need who are using the services, if this is possible, but most will represent absolute increase. There is no point in carrying out publicity until this increase in demand, and the likely call on resources, is estimated and catered for.' The Research and Intelligence Unit, charged with the duty of answering the question 'What is the size of this unmet need and therefore the extra resources that would be required to meet it?' is saying that it cannot start a publicity campaign to identify the size of this unmet need, and therefore the extra resources required to meet it until the increase in demand and the likely call on resources has been estimated and catered for. By whom?

The report concludes by recommending four studies. The first would be a statement of the objectives and operational criteria by which departments determine those in need. 'This is important in itself to be clear about, but also necessary as a step toward measuring need,' it says. If its intention is to do no more than study present definitions of need, and only in relation to the services the local authority can supply, then I find it restricted in its aims. It would be much more valuable to state definitions of all forms of need whether local authority services are involved or not.

The second study recommended was to look at the problem of why old people in need do not come forward, the reasons providing the basis for planning any publicity campaign in the future. This would certainly provide interesting information, but again it refers to the publicity campaign which I believe starts from entirely the wrong premise.

The third study was on the case records that departments keep. This would attempt to describe the characteristics of old people who were being helped and was 'an essential step towards this survey'.

Finally, the Research and Intelligence Unit intended, when all this had been successfully carried out, to carry out a survey of unmet need in 1972.

This report, as I mentioned earlier, studied a number of previous surveys, but pointed out that many were probably now out of date and that they offered little help in projecting future provisions. However, a number of general conclusions from them were reached.

One was: 'The variety in the provision of services in no way compares with the variety of needs – this applies particularly to hostels, homes and housing.' If this is the case, and all the evidence suggests that it is, then it is argued that a statement of the objectives and operational criteria by which departments determine those in need is less relevant than an overall study of the extent of need and the types of need, because, obviously, local authority departments must determine need to fit the provision they can make. And, the conclusion is, the variety of that provision in no way compares to the variety of needs.

Another conclusion was: 'Many of those determined as being in great need either do not recognize (or will not admit) the need themselves – or if they do admit it *say* they would not use local authority services.'

If this is a conclusion which the Research and Intelligence Unit believes is correct, and again there is no reason to doubt its validity, then its proposal to use publicity to seek out unmet need, which has the 'advantage' of excluding those who would not welcome help, is nonsense. The kind of people who do not recognize (or will not admit) that they need help, or merely say that they would not use local authority services, would be hardly likely to respond to a publicity campaign. Yet these are very often the people who most need help.

This report contains one major omission. It offers no comment on means of answering the question 'How is need likely to grow in the future and what system could be developed to monitor this growth?' Accurate statistics of the present total need will help make good projections for the future, but a system for monitoring the growth of need is more difficult.

In identifying need and monitoring it Seebohm talked of 'co-operation and understanding at all levels of the community', and the greatest value of publicity is to achieve greater understanding and cooperation. In my view, if manpower is the problem in doing a proper door-to-door survey, then the assistance of voluntary organizations will have to be sought. Many of them have great experience and they have workers who are well able to make an assessment of the problems they encounter. If such assessments are beyond them, then they should be able to refer the case to the medical authorities or to trained social workers. 'Voluntary organizations pioneered social service reform in the past and we see them playing a major role in developing citizen participation in *revealing new needs** and in exposing shortcomings in the services,' said Seebohm.

It seems to me that no survey in which professional work is restricted by manpower and expense can be fully successful. Either it will be a sample survey or it will concentrate on one district alone, when what is required is accurate, overall identification and assessment which will put every old person in need of help in touch with an agency which can assist. To do this properly must mean the involvement of voluntary organizations and individuals who are qualified and willing to help. But it may well be that comprehensive surveys of this kind will not be possible until social-service departments are properly reorganized and working in a much more useful partnership with voluntary organizations than at present. I would suggest that one of the ways in which citizen participation can be encouraged is in helping in such a survey. In this type of work there is no substitute for 'door-knocking'.

In criticizing the Research and Intelligence Unit for suggest-

Author's italics.

ing that the discovery of unmet need can be made through publicity I speak from the experience gained by *The Star* during 1970. Our main purpose was to try to find solutions for those with problems and we asked needy people or those who knew of needy people to contact us. While this produced well over a thousand cases on our records, there is no guarantee that this reached every old person in need.

Furthermore, I doubt whether methods of publicity devised by a Research and Intelligence unit could be as effective as those used by an evening newspaper with a circulation of nearly 200,000 which, at a conservative estimate, is read by 600,000 people and which asked to be told of lonely and needy old people six days a week for a whole year. The information derived from the reported cases was valuable only after the reports had been followed up and the people concerned had been visited. I also wonder what attitude the local authority would adopt towards anonymous and sometimes illiterate requests for help, inarticulate pleas which told little of the circumstances involved.

Publicity produces many new cases of unmet need, but discovering the extent and variety of that need means field work and manpower. Publicity can help but I do not believe there is any substitute for having workers on the ground. If research and intelligence units and the social services do not have the manpower or the money to do such a survey, then they must seek the help of volunteers. Certainly the early detection of new cases and the monitoring of future need will depend very largely on voluntary workers, particularly early detection, which not only needs established voluntary organizations but increased citizen participation.

Fourteen

Conclusion

Perhaps the first conclusion that has to be drawn from this account is that there are areas of the country – the industrial towns and cities with their backlog of Industrial Revolution dereliction – with special problems to solve if they are to improve substantially their provisions for the old. As we have seen the quality and quantity of services to the aged varies greatly from area to area and, in my view, the big urban authorities like Sheffield, with considerable remaining problems of slum clearance and urban renewal and extensive waiting lists for old people's flats and places in residential homes, ought to receive special government help to solve them. Sheffield has attacked its slums without respite since the war and yet is years away from solving its housing problem; it has expanded its social services continually, but finds itself hard pressed in making more and better provision. Furthermore, its financial difficulties include a fairly static rateable value. The income from a penny rate (£97,852 in 1969–70) has been about the same for a number of years, and increased revenue to pay for better services means an increase in the rate poundage. In such circumstances there is a case for selective central government help in building for old people and expanding welfare services for them.

If the present Government is committed to a policy of selectivity – giving help where it is most needed – it will, however, demand proof of need. Such proof, where it relates to the care of the elderly, can only be revealed by thorough investigation.

As I have already argued, we need to know more about the circumstances of old people in each local authority area for which a social services committee is responsible. This will not only provide proof of need for special help, but will also provide the statistical information for forward planning on a local basis. Under no circumstances must investigation be restricted by considerations such as unwillingness to accept help and ineligibility to receive local authority services. Any surveys into the condition of old people must be comprehensive. They must aim to provide information which will be of use to every organization concerned with the welfare of the elderly and not just the local authority.

Implicit in research into the nature and extent of distress among the elderly is the gathering of opinions about social services and housing by the consumers. 'In the provision of social services the users are seldom consulted,' said Seebohm. Had the users been consulted and their opinions heeded more effort might have gone into providing flats without access staircases and more sheltered housing schemes. I regard the failure to provide enough of the proper types of housing for old people as the most serious gap in our statutory services for the old. This situation must be improved urgently. In saying this, I realize the financial difficulties and how soaring costs can throw current plans into confusion.

An example in December 1970 was when Sheffield Housing Committee learned from its officers that a £138,000 contract for forty old people's flatlets and six flats would have to be re-negotiated because the price had gone way above the Government's cost yardstick. A yardstick increase of five per cent in April 1969 and another five per cent in April 1970 had failed to keep pace with increases in the price of building materials. Such a situation can jeopardize a local authority's building programme and for an authority like Sheffield to substantially increase its building for old people without special help from central government will be a formidable task.

It is one of the most unfortunate facts of life that the design of old people's flats is related to the cost and that the better designs seem to be more expensive. Sheffield already has far too many flats for old people with access staircases and intends to build more. In my view no more such designs should be included in the building programme and the City should demand that its architects produce designs more suitable for the old. It is also high time that some civic leaders stopped defending staircase designs and admitted they have been wrong.

As I have intended to show, access to the statutory social services is not as easy as it might be. I am convinced that local authorities must set up central points where people may go for help and advice with social problems. Sheffield decided to investigate such a central agency in February 1970, but by December nothing further had been heard, a lamentable example of how slowly local government can work, even when faced with an urgent problem. When people do not know what services are available and how they can be assisted by them, such a central office is essential.

Seebohm said:

Many of those submitting evidence stressed the difficulty which the public and members of other services found in approaching the local authority personal social services. People are often unclear about the pattern of services and uncertain about the division of responsibilities between them. Initially a person's true need (sometimes a matter for expert diagnosis) may not be clearly recognized: sometimes the person seeking help may be confused and inarticulate and unable to make plain what particular help he requires. In such circumstances it may be difficult for him to get straight to the right services and the delay and further referral this involves may be discouraging, particularly if the local offices of different services are a considerable distance apart. Furthermore members of the public are often diffident about approaching the services, either on their own behalf, or on behalf of relatives or acquaintances. They may doubt whether help is available or they may fear officials to be remote and bureaucratic.

Undoubtedly a fear of bureaucracy and a feeling that when presented with problems the local authority will not take action exist. We received many complaints from the public that their requests and problems were not dealt with urgently. To see a four-year-old letter from the Housing Department informing an old couple that they had been granted medical priority for rehousing and that their case would not be overlooked, and then to learn this was their last communication from the Department, does not lead one to think the administration of services is efficient enough.

To give the public single referral points where they could take such problems and be sympathetically advised and informed would go a long way towards allaying fears of remote bureaucracy. Such a centre would perform an even more valuable function if it could also put people in touch with voluntary services on a district basis. Giving the public a place to take their troubles is one of the things local authorities must aim for with much more urgency than Sheffield demonstrated in 1970.

For thousands of old people who live alone accident or illness can strike suddenly. Sometimes they can lie for hours, perhaps until death, without anyone knowing. Therefore they should have some means of summoning help in an emergency. At the beginning of 1970 none of Sheffield's council flats for old people had alarms with which to call the help of either neighbours or wardens. The Corporation decided to install alarm systems, wherever practical, in October 1970, but, even when undertaken as a matter of urgency, it will be some time before this work is completed and of course it will not be possible to fit alarms in every flat. In the meantime, the Corporation and the *Telegraph* and *Star* Old Folk's Fund organized a public appeal to buy portable, battery-operated alarms for the 19,000 (estimated) old people who live alone in Sheffield. Such alarms will be the only security for those who live alone in private property.

Many suggestions have been made about the best and cheapest way of informing neighbours that an old person is in distress and needs help. These have ranged from tear-off calendars in the window where the wrong date is a warning to flashing alarm lights and alarms connected to toilet flush mechanisms – if the normal bodily functions are not performed regularly then the old persons must need help. Alarms are best linked to a warden service. But even a link to a warden's flat is not a guarantee that help will come if, after a fall, the old person cannot reach a button or pull-cord. Portable, battery-operated alarms have the advantage of being small enough to be carried in a pocket and with batteries cost less than 30p. When activated by pressing a button or pulling out a small pin they produce a penetrating note loud enough for neighbours or passers-by to hear in normal circumstances and will sound continuously until the battery runs down – about forty-five minutes. Like a fixed alarm system, they are not ideal (nor is any form of alarm) but they have already been used successfully and give old people living alone an added sense of security in the knowledge that they can summon help in an emergency. In future all groupings of old folk's flats ought to be fitted with some form of alarm system, preferably one which connects with a warden's quarters.

If, as I believe, the successful care of the elderly rests just as much on a firm community foundation as it does on a base of statutory welfare services, then communities must not only be encouraged in their development and the establishment of identity, but must also be encouraged to play a real part in the decision-making processes which affect them. It is clear that they have had too little influence in the past and that a general attitude which says it is useless for them to argue with the authorities persists.

Changes, however, are taking place. I am pleased to see that in Sheffield strong community action groups have been formed which are determined to influence Corporation plans for their areas. In December 1970, under the title Sheffield's Grass Roots, five community action groups published a report which criticized the Corporation for failing to consult sufficiently with communities in its redevelopment plans for Sheffield's inner, older area. The editor of the report, Geoffrey Green, a research student at Sheffield University, said that the Skeffington Committee Report, *People and Planning*, had now become a handbook for Sheffield's action groups and commented:

Any group of residents organized to carry Report's recommendations through to particular areas of Sheffield is regarded by the

175

City's opinion leaders initially and generally as 'a good thing'. The crunch comes when they begin to tackle specific problems and inevitably bring themselves into conflict with the local authority, both councillors and officials.

For by simply pointing to the lack of consultation over, say, the design and type of new Corporation housing, or in the slum clearance process, Action Groups implicitly criticize the way in which the Local Authority presently operates. And only naturally the first reaction of those who made the decisions is to defend themselves completely. Individual councillors will suggest quite rightly but irrelevantly that they have responded to every problem raised by individual constituents, and committee chairmen will point (missing the point) to Sheffield's remarkable post-war housing record.

He agreed that Sheffield's controlling Labour Group had gone a long way towards accepting the need for public participation and a little way towards putting it into effect, but concluded that Corporation initiatives to ensure maximum public involvement had not been enough.

His complaint against the local authority, in the light of his experience with action groups, was exactly the one which I have emphasized in this book : that the local authority has stressed the physical in its Town Planning without taking sufficient stock of social change.

Mr Green suggested that Sheffield Corporation should appoint a team of sociologists or social scientists to work on the demolition as well as the design stages of redevelopment, and also to appoint a planning communications officer to organize the dialogue between planners and planned.

While this would help towards greater understanding of the problems and could lead to better communications, it would be more valuable for the Corporation to take a long hard look at what it is doing in the city's inner area of redevelopment in an attempt to keep people in such areas and to preserve their communities. I have long contended that people, especially the old, do not wish to be rehoused on the outskirts on sometimes hilly, windy estates, where winter can seem doubly hard, and the Walkley Action Group provided statistical confirmation of this view.

In a survey it conducted, completed questionnaires were re-turned from 1,545 households of whom only sixteen per cent wanted to leave the district altogether. Sixty-two per cent wan-ted to stay where they were, if necessary with their houses improved, and a further twenty-two per cent also wanted to stay in Walkley. This survey revealed that only twenty-five per cent of households had both bathrooms and indoor lavatories and that here there was a great disparity between owner-occupiers and those who rented. Forty-five per cent of owner-occupiers had both bath and indoor lavatory, facilities which only seven per cent of those who rented enjoyed. Two thirds of the over-sixties age group lived in rented houses whereas youn-ger households were evenly split between owning and renting.

The report comments: 'One thing stood out very clearly: Walkley is a very stable community – over half the renters and a third of all owner-occupiers had lived there for over twenty years'. This fact confirms my own assertion that the most stable elements in slum clearance communities are the elderly and middle-aged.

Action Group secretary Robin Stanford wrote:

We have got a fascinating picture of Walkley but we are not sure exactly how our survey can be used to guide the planners' work. All that we have been able to do is to prove our original point that wholesale demolition in Walkley is absolutely wrong; there are still no signs that the planners are interested in the information or that having got it they would know how to use it.

Apart from what it revealed about the people who make up a slum clearance community, this survey also deserved notice because it showed how much social study can be done by a team of enthusiasts, about forty strong, some of whom were Sheffield University students. However, is it not the duty of the local authority to undertake such social investigation when it is considering dispossessing and uprooting thousands of people? Surely such a survey, combined with the fullest expression of local opinion is a prerequisite long before the City's planners embark on grandiose redevelopment plans. This survey also shows that in investigating the condition of the elderly in

Sheffield there are voluntary interests which can be called upon for assistance.

It is through community action of this nature that better care for old people can come – the difficulties of housing the elderly and providing them with adequate statutory social services will be with us for many years to come even if selectivity and giving greater government aid where it is most needed lead to faster developments in the urban problem-areas. Certainly, it is to the community that we must look to provide a greater measure of more immediate care for the aged.

Better services in the way of housing, health and welfare, and a pension which bears a reasonable relationship to the cost of living, must be complemented by the companionship of being part of a community, in whatever sense one wishes to interpret the word. For example, those old people who need help but who are chary of accepting it from the local authority may be more disposed to be helped by the local community. And if old people are properly to have their independence preserved there is much that the community can do. However, local authorities like Sheffield must make a more vigorous attempt to set up area voluntary organizations, possibly based on existing community associations, with the declared object of reaching every old and handicapped person in the area. This should extend down to the level of volunteer wardens who would be close to the old people in their streets. Such area organizations could coordinate the work presently done by voluntary organizations, churches, youth clubs, good-neighbour schemes, schools, etc., and have proper liaison with the statutory services. In this way the circumstances of all old people in an area could be investigated, great knowledge would be gained and regular contact would ensure that help could be given quickly as soon as physical or mental deterioration began to affect an old person.

This would be the only way of investigating *all* cases and likely cases of need, providing an early warning system at the same time. I cannot stress too strongly the importance of reaching old people before their need becomes desperate and their circumstances distressed or neglected. When their need becomes desperate, when their physical or mental deterioration has reached the point where they are at risk and only then are they discovered, society has failed them.

In encouraging community action and increasing public participation in services for the old, it is necessary that people are made truly aware of the nature and extent of the problems our pensioners face. By describing, publicizing and reporting in depth on numerous cases of social distress (including those of people who were not necessarily old) *The Star* carried out a valuable public service in Sheffield in 1970. Its exposures put pressure on the local authority to seek means of improving services to the old in planning for more old folk's homes, more sheltered flatlet schemes, to increase its welfare staff, to reconsider the design of flats for old people and to seek ways of improving liaison with voluntary organizations. Furthermore, it created a climate of opinion in which, because the public were aware that improved services would cost more money, a substantial increase in rates provoked surprisingly little adverse comment (in an editorial the newspaper commented that the rise had not been big enough!).

To do this requires a strong, vigorous local newspaper with sufficient senior and experienced staff to investigate thoroughly and draw conclusions. *The Star* is quite clearly in the position described by Dilys M. Hill in *Participating in Local Affairs*, when she said:

The evening newspapers make the largest contribution to community debate because they offer a continuous stream of information. They can afford the staff and the space for civic affairs. They are situated in the larger towns in which the local authority is an important source of interesting news. The importance and range of local services in these towns, and the sound commercial position of the newspapers results in better reporting ...

... The picture of the local paper as an avenue of protest and a source of information has greater reality in large towns than in small communities. In general, the citizen of these larger communities enjoys a better service from his newspaper. Larger newspapers can be independent of the council's attitudes because they obtain information from a variety of sources and do not rely solely on council minutes. This is an important consideration; so few authorities promote any publicity campaigns, and the individual who wants to discover more about local affairs is therefore dependent on the press.

In these circumstances a local newspaper has an important role to play in civic affairs. It can stimulate widespread discussion on topics of vital public interest; it can be the catalyst in promoting action to remedy social injustices. At a time when action groups are demanding for the public greater participation in the decision-making processes of local government, the local newspaper has a greater duty than ever before to provide the public with information and opinions to help their deliberations. Certainly, when the topic is one of such importance as the care of old people it has a duty to dig deep into the facts and the background and provide its readers with more information, and more opinion upon that information than would be elucidated by mere recourse to official sources.

In my opinion, despite the pressure exerted on the local authority by *The Star* and the steps which were taken as a result, the newspaper's greatest contribution to the care of the old in Sheffield in 1970 was to make people more aware that a grave social problem, which needed their participation in its solution, existed in their midst.

Anthropologists have made studies which relate human behaviour to that of animals, and their conclusion is often that it is the fittest who survive. Early man was forced by the harsh circumstances of his existence to struggle with others to survive and to some extent this is still shown in man's inhumanity to man. Like the beasts, early man procreated to ensure the survival of the species, guarding his children above all else, and even in this century there are primitive tribes which cast out the old and leave them to die once their usefulness to the community has been ended by old age and infirmity: the nomadic warrior Masai of East Africa are an example. Were modern man through overpopulation and hunger to be faced with a decision whether to cast out the old so that his children would survive and the species be continued, I feel certain that we would make the same choice as if we were still living in primitive conditions in which only the fittest survive.

But we live in a modern, affluent, developed and developing society in which we have no good excuses for neglecting our old people. To leave them alone, uncared for, isolated from the world in depressing slums, at risk from the winter's cold, is our equivalent of casting them out once their usefulness to society is over. Society, of course, can make its excuses. Arguments about inflation, stagnation, balances of payment, external debts, gross national product and the economic state of the nation are just that – excuses. What is in fact being excused is a political failure to manage the economy in a way which gives social justice to the underprivileged of this country among whom the elderly are the most numerous and the least powerful.

I find it a matter of the gravest injustice that, while thousands of pensioners struggle to pay for winter fuel and food and many face death from cold, it is widely quoted that eighty per cent of the country's wealth is in the hands of a mere two per cent of the population. What is needed is radical political reform to redistribute the wealth of the nation for the benefit of the people as a whole. Until such political action brings an end to social injustice the needs of the elderly are unlikely to be given sufficient priority and the plight of Britain's old folk will continue to be on our conscience.

Appendix
An Insight into Old Age

By Danny Gallagher

What does life hold for the thousands of old people who live alone, confined by their infirmities? The answer is – very little. It is hard for us to imagine the degree of boredom and isolation that narrows their lives, the drag of the hours until the evening television programmes bring relief, and the pathetic, trusting dependence on the few visitors who call.

To investigate the life of a lonely pensioner, my colleague Danny Gallagher lived with an old man for two weeks, sharing his isolation and examining the problems which confronted him.

This is his report:

Mr C. was typical of many pensioners who are housebound through infirmity. He was helped by the social services, he received other visitors, he had television, and yet his life was monotonous and drab. He was in no way physically neglected, but the difficulties he faced represented the problems that beset thousands. Aged seventy-three, he had been a widower for six years after a childless marriage. His nearest relative was a seventy-nine-year-old brother who lived at Whitby, and was too far away and too old himself to visit.

Three years before Mr C. had suffered a stroke and as a result had gradually lost the use of his left side. His partial paralysis meant he could no longer get out and about. He lived in a terraced house not far from the city centre in one of the older parts of the city. It was a two-up, two-down house, with a lavatory at the bottom of the back yard. After twenty years in the house he was reluctant to leave its familiarity and refused the offer of a place in a residential home.

His working life started at the age of thirteen when he was taken on by a Sheffield firm as an apprentice silversmith. Three months later he changed his mind about his future occupation and became an apprentice plumber employed by an uncle. He served for three years in the Royal Flying Corps at Farnborough and on discharge returned to Sheffield to spend three months in a sheet metal works before moving to the maintenance department of the Royal Victoria Hotel, where he worked until the age of seventy.

Mr C. had more visitors than many lonely old people. His greatest friend was a former colleague from the hotel who called regularly during the week. His other callers included a visitor from a local church, occasionally the vicar, and two other friends. Each day a home help came for at least an hour. At one time the home help only came once a week but, as his disability worsened, her visits became more frequent.

A typical day in his life began at 6 a.m. when he would wake up and switch on the portable radio at the side of his bed. Like many old people he awoke early and would lie in bed for at least an hour, listening to the radio before attempting to get out of bed. It would take him at least twenty minutes to get dressed, using only his right arm – his left hung limp at his side. Using an electric torch he would fumble his way into the passage where the room light-switch was located. While on his feet he would go through into the back kitchen to collect the morning paper from his letter box. He would sit and glance over the headlines while on the gas stove a pan of water boiled ready for his morning brew of tea.

The home help was usually his first caller. She would not only make his bed, in the living room, but would tidy the room, wash dishes and go to the local shop for his groceries.

Once she was gone he was back to reading his paper, which was the only thing he had to occupy his mind until television programmes began in the late afternoon. He would watch until just after 8 p.m., his normal bedtime. Getting undressed for bed was again an uncomfortable struggle.

His normal lunch would be a plate of sandwiches prepared by the home help before she left. He usually saved some for his tea. Because of his disability he found it difficult to prepare cooked meals and Sunday lunch was usually his only hot meal of the week.

Because of his partial paralysis his movements were slow and unsteady. Wherever he moved around the house he had to reach out for chairs and cupboards for support. He fell many times and in reaching out to save himself had smashed the glass fronts of two cabinets. If things he needed were not on the kitchen shelf he had to take the risk of getting them from a cellar-head pantry perched high above nine steps. One slip could have meant a dangerous fall to the cellar below. Coal for the fire in the kitchen was stored in the cellar but, because he could not get down to bring it up, he had no fire. The home help had offered to bring it up for him but he refused her offer because he did not want to create extra work for her.

His frequent falls had a shattering effect on his morale. He had gradually lost confidence in his ability to walk and daily became more confined to his front room. His most serious fall occurred on Christmas Eve 1969. He was unable to get up from the floor and had to spend the night lying covered only by a blanket he had managed to pull from the bed. It was well into Christmas morning before he regained enough strength to pull himself to his feet.

While I was staying with him he had another bad fall when on his way into the kitchen. If I had not been there to help him to his feet and back to his bed he would probably have lain there until the home help arrived at least an hour later.

His disability could have been eased to an extent by the fitting of handrails along the walls in both the living room, the passageway and kitchen. It would also have been a help to have the switches for both lights and television at the side of his bed.

After his stroke he spent a year in hospital but both he and his visitors expressed the view that further therapeutic treatment as an out-patient could have eased his infirmity. While I was staying with him a health visitor called and suggested that he should have more exercise and that she would make arrangements for him to attend a day centre.

Attendance at a day centre would also help to break the tedium of his daily routine. For him life was a series of long, uneventful days. When he was discharged from hospital he found he still had some use in his left hand and occupied his time by repairing watches. He found then that his days were not so lonely. At the same time he could still walk fairly well with the aid of a stick, and used to be able to make his way to the local shop and cafe to meet people and pass the time of day. When his paralysis worsened he found he could no longer enjoy the pastime of watch-repairing, nor could he leave the house.

Eventually he was reduced to spending long and lonely days either sitting or lying on his bed in the living-room where in winter the gas fire was on all day. In common with many old people, he liked to reminisce. The angling cups on his cabinet took him back to the days when he used to compete in club matches and angling was then his favourite hobby.

Every day he would read his morning paper from cover to cover as though he were memorizing every word. I have also seen him stretched out on his bed for hours on end just staring at the ceiling. His eyes were focused there, but his thoughts were not.

His whole life was centred on the television set and each afternoon was anxiously spent awaiting the time when the set could be switched on. On many occasions he would turn it on when all that was shown was the test card. He found company in the music which helped break the silence of the room. No matter what programme was showing he would watch it. He was not at all selective in his viewing, and though he often expressed dislike for a certain programme he would watch it all the same.

He kept a pet, a black and white cat, and gave it lavish attention. In this respect he was very typical of most lonely pensioners. They cling to a pet for company, showering it with affection but receiving little in return. At night the cat would venture into the living-room but throughout the day it would usually sleep under a chair in the kitchen, oblivious to its master's frequent calls. He often said he would have preferred a dog for greater companionship but he could not have one because he could not exercise it.

Spending two weeks in the home of a lonely pensioner had an important effect on me. As a result of my personal experience I was better able to understand what true loneliness is and what effect it has on an old person.

Each day was so uneventful that it seemed interminable. Nothing happened, and it happened all the time. There were times when I wanted to put on my coat and go out of the door and walk for miles. I must admit that at first I looked on the two weeks I spent with the old man as a prison sentence and was anxiously awaiting the time when I would be free. But then I realized that, although I was to live this life of seclusion for only a short period, he and the many pensioners like him would experience nothing else for the rest of their lives. It was a frightening thought. The most depressing thing was sitting looking out of the window at the people hurrying past. There was at the most six feet between us but it might just as well have been six miles. The old man was all too well aware that his daily routine was simple and repetitive and twice I saw him break down and weep at the sheer futility of it all.

In his case there seemed little that anyone could do to break the monotony. One friend called each week to see if he was fit to be taken out for a car ride, but of course he was not. This constant reminder of his disability had a depressing effect on him. His other visitors brought only temporary relief from his loneliness. Once they were gone it was back with renewed force.

Because he had led an active life until the age of seventy, his confinement was all the more unbearable. An important factor which had a great bearing on his outlook was the fact that because of the death of his wife he had no constant companion to share his tedious hours. Reference to his wife always brought a tear to his eye.

A few days after my fortnight with him ended, he had another serious fall after which he was admitted to hospital. Again he had to spend all night on the floor before his home help arrived and found him.

Quite clearly, instead of continuing his struggle at home, he would have been better housed in a warden-supervised flatlet scheme, where he could have retained a degree of independence and at the same time had the companionship of other people around him and the constant help of a warden. The only other solution was a place in a residential home, which was unacceptable to him, since he wished to retain his independence.

For me, the two weeks provided a premature insight into old age. What I found was not very pleasant, but far more unpleasant was the reminder it brought that this is what lies at the end of the road for far too many of us.

More about Penguins and Pelicans

Penguinews, which appears every month, contains details of all the new books issued by Penguins as they are published. From time to time it is supplemented by *Penguins in Print*, which is a complete list of all books published by Penguins which are in print. (There are well over three thousand of these.)

A specimen copy of *Penguinews* will be sent to you free on request, and you can become a subscriber for the price of the postage. For a year's issues (including the complete lists) please send 30p if you live in the United Kingdom, or 60p if you live elsewhere. Just write to Dept EP, Penguin Books Ltd, Harmondsworth, Middlesex, enclosing a cheque or postal order, and your name will be added to the mailing list.

Note : *Penguinews* and *Penguins in Print* are not available in the U.S.A. or Canada

The Psychology of Human Ageing

D. B. Bromley

Infant and adolescent psychology have been very
thoroughly explored : but the study of ageing lags behind.

A gerontologist, who is scientific adviser in this field
to the Medical Research Council, fills a gap in the
literature of psychology with this new introduction to
human ageing and its mental effects. Dealing with the
course of life from maturity onwards, Dr Bromley
examines many biological and social effects of human
ageing ; personality and adjustment ; mental disorders
in adult life and old age ; age changes in the organization
of occupational and skilled performance ; adult
intelligence ; and age changes in intellectual, social, and
other achievements. A final section on method in the
study of ageing makes this book an important
contribution for the student of psychology as well as the
layman.

A Pelican Original

Poverty: The Forgotten Englishman

Ken Coates and Richard Silburn

Is poverty in Britain a thing of the past? Too many
of our countrymen regularly do without the minimum
considered necessary for a healthy diet; they live in houses
that are overcrowded, insanitary and ludicrously
expensive to keep warm and comfortable; their children
attend schools in which teaching is a near impossibility.

Ken Coates and Richard Silburn look again at what is
meant by the word 'poverty'. They conclude that vast
numbers of Englishmen, living in slums throughout the
country, are, for most of their lives, living in acute
poverty. What this actually involves is spelled out by
means of a detailed survey of one slum: St Ann's in
Nottingham, which is typical of hundreds of such
districts.

The book continues with a study of welfare services and
why they fail to alleviate or remove poverty. Finally
there is an analysis of the frequent failure of slum-
clearance schemes and a discussion of new alternatives.

This disturbing Penguin Special attacks a problem – the
problem of modern urban poverty – which western
society has neglected, is neglecting, but will only go on
neglecting at its peril.

Another Penguin Special